AF255493

Navigating Emotions in Digital Thinking Classrooms: A Guide to Social and Emotional Learning

Building Emotional Intelligence and Connection in Digital Education

Jocelyn Dimaala

Dedication

For the students who arrive curious, the teachers who keep showing up, and the families who steady the work—may this book help you name what you feel, choose your next step, and stay connected across every screen and classroom.

For my mentors and colleagues who taught me that compassion and clarity belong together—this is for the small, steady moves that make learning human.

And to my family: for patience, belief, and every conversation that reminded me why this work matters.

Acknowledgment

First and always, my deepest thanks to Almighty God—source of wisdom, strength, and steadying light. Your gracious presence has guided this work; may these pages serve others as a small reflection of that care.

To the teachers: this book exists because of you. Thank you for your patience, creativity, and quiet courage. You turn research into routines, keep classrooms humane when systems wobble, and make the small, repeatable moves that let learning—and belonging—take root, whether on a screen or in person. Thank you for testing ideas in real classrooms, for telling the truth about what worked and what didn't, and for welcoming students with care every day. Your feedback shaped these pages; your perseverance makes the work of SEL possible.

To my colleagues, mentors, and the many community partners who shared their time, expertise, and encouragement—your insight and support strengthened the ideas presented here. To the families who partner with schools and model resilience at home, thank you for the everyday practices that teach children how to steady themselves and one another.

Finally, to the students whose voices remind us why this matters: your curiosity, courage, and capacity to grow are the reason we keep trying.

With deep gratitude to everyone who showed up, listened, and kept the work human.

About the Author

Jocelyn Dimaala is an accomplished school leader and principal whose career is devoted to the intersection of education, technology, and sustainability. With a strong passion for robotics and artificial intelligence, she leverages her diverse experience across education, business outsourcing, food and beverage, and manufacturing sectors to bring a multifaceted perspective to her work. During her immersion program in the US, she pioneered a "Math with a Heart" classbook, blending academic rigor with compassion. She is a dedicated advocate for Social and Emotional Learning (SEL) in the classroom, supporting students' holistic development.

As a globally recognized sustainability ambassador and advocate for Industry 5.0 and Women in Tech, Jocelyn actively promotes environmental consciousness and inclusive empowerment. She serves in key roles such as Ambassador Pro for the Global School Alliance and Climate Action Project, and as country chair for Academia within the Global Sustainable Futures Network. Her numerous accolades—including the Women in Tech APAC Global Leadership Award, Education International Outstanding Leadership Award, America's Role Model Sustainability Iconic Award, and recognition as a top ESG and Green Tech influencer in Asia—highlight her commitment to driving meaningful change through technology and collaboration, especially in empowering women and youth.

Jocelyn is also the visionary founder of the Global SDG Quest network. This pioneering international initiative uses game-based learning to deepen understanding of the UN's Sustainable Development Goals in over 50 schools across 20 countries. Beyond her leadership and innovation, she is an international speaker, sharing insights on design thinking, digital literacy, leadership, educational technology, and global classroom strategies at prestigious conferences worldwide. Her inspiring motto, "Together we learn, sustain, and transform the world," embodies her dedication to fostering unity and sustainable progress through education.

Source: www.linkedin.com/in/msjocelynd

Preface

Classrooms have always been more than rooms. They are the sum of small, steady moments: a name remembered, a pause to clarify, a chance to try again without losing face. When learning moved onto screens, those moments didn't disappear—they just became easier to miss. This book began as a simple commitment to notice them again and to rebuild, on purpose, the human layer of digital learning.

What follows is practical by design. I've tried to keep the theory light and the moves repeatable: a one-minute check-in that lowers the cost of speaking; shared roles that make group work fair; short "reset" pauses that help attention return after a glitch or a knock at the door; two-question self-assessments that teach students to steer their own progress. None of these requires new software or long training. They require clarity, consistency, and respect for how real students actually live and learn online.

The book opens with foundations—what social and emotional learning (SEL) really asks of us, and why it matters in digital spaces—then shifts quickly to the grain of classroom life: routines that make participation safe, language for repairing misreads in chat, ways to honor multiple paths of contribution (voice, camera, text, short posts).

You'll find guidance for partnering with families without flooding them, assessing SEL lightly so it informs rather than labels, and keeping equity central when bandwidth, devices, or privacy are uneven.

I've also looked ahead. Tools will change—AI, mixed reality, new platforms—but the work will stay the same: help students know what they feel, choose a next step, listen for what others carry, and act with care in shared spaces. When we get those habits into the daily rhythm of a course, grades improve, yes—but so do belonging, confidence, and the willingness to keep going when the work is hard.

If this book helps you recover a few of those small moments and make them routine again, it has done its job. The aim is not perfection. The aim is a class that feels steady and human enough for real learning to take root—online, in person, or anywhere we meet.

Contents

Chapter 1: Introduction

In today's world, it sometimes feels like the ground beneath our feet is shifting faster than we can catch our balance. Technology is not just changing how we live, but is also reshaping the way we learn, teach, and connect with one another.

Education, in particular, has undergone one of the most dramatic shifts. Classrooms are no longer limited by four walls and rows of desks. Now, they extend into our homes, coffee shops, libraries, and sometimes even our pockets through mobile devices.

This transformation has opened exciting new possibilities. Students can collaborate with peers worldwide, teachers can share resources instantly, and learning can occur at any time of day. But as doors open to new opportunities, another reality comes into focus: digital learning, for all its benefits, also brings challenges that touch the heart of who we are as human beings.

At its core, education has always been about more than memorizing facts or passing exams. It's about preparing young people to step into the world with confidence, resilience, and the ability to work with others. It's about helping them discover their strengths, learn to manage their struggles, and develop empathy for those around them. In other words, education is as much an emotional journey as it is an intellectual one. And that's where Social and Emotional Learning, or SEL, becomes so important.

SEL isn't new. Teachers have always been aware that students' feelings, relationships, and sense of self shape how they learn. What is new is the urgency with which we must bring SEL into digital classrooms. Screens can connect us, but they can also create distance. Online spaces can feel liberating, but they can also leave students feeling isolated or unseen.

Navigating these complexities requires intentional effort from educators, families, and communities. This book explores the effort to create digital classrooms that are not only places of knowledge but also spaces where emotional intelligence flourishes.

The Importance of SEL in Digital Classrooms

So, what exactly is Social and Emotional Learning? At its simplest, SEL is the process of developing the skills we need to understand and manage our emotions, build healthy relationships, make thoughtful decisions, and cope with challenges.

The Collaborative for Academic, Social, and Emotional Learning (CASEL) defines SEL through five core competencies: self-awareness, self-management, social awareness, relationship skills, and responsible decision-making (CASEL, 2023)[1].

When we think about these skills in the context of a digital classroom, their importance becomes even clearer. Imagine a student logging into an online lesson. There are no hallways buzzing with conversation, no desks arranged in small groups,

---

[1] **CASEL.** (n.d.). *Fundamentals of SEL.* Retrieved from https://casel.org/fundamentals-of-sel/

no subtle cues from body language or facial expressions that help them feel connected. Instead, there's a screen, i.e., a window that can either connect them or make them feel more alone. In that space, a student's ability to regulate emotions, express themselves clearly, and empathize with others becomes not just helpful but essential.

Research has shown time and again that SEL is not an "extra" to education, but a foundation that supports learning. A large-scale meta-analysis found that students who participated in SEL programs saw an 11 percentile-point gain in academic performance compared with their peers who did not (Durlak et al., 2011)[2].

That's a striking figure because it reminds us that emotions and academics are deeply connected. When students feel supported emotionally, they are more likely to engage, persevere, and succeed.

But SEL isn't just about boosting test scores. It's also about long-term well-being. Another study showed that the positive effects of SEL programs, like better social skills, improved attitudes, and reduced conduct problems, can last for years after the intervention ends (Taylor et al., 2017)[3].

---

[2] Durlak, J. A., Weissberg, R. P., Dymnicki, A. B., Taylor, R. D., & Schellinger, K. B. (2011). *The impact of enhancing students' social and emotional learning: A meta-analysis of school-based universal interventions. Child Development, 82*(1), 405–432. https://doi.org/10.1111/j.1467-8624.2010.01564.x

[3] Taylor, R. D., Oberle, E., Durlak, J. A., & Weissberg, R. P. (2017). *Promoting positive youth development through school-based social and emotional learning interventions: A meta-analysis of follow-up effects. Child Development, 88*(4), 1156-1171. https://doi.org/10.1111/cdev.12864

This means that when we take SEL seriously in schools, we're not only helping students today, but also preparing them for the future. It helps shape their futures as adults who can work effectively with others, manage stress, and make positive contributions to their communities.

Now, consider what happens when these principles are applied in digital learning spaces. Online learning can be flexible, but it also creates unique challenges. For example:

- **Isolation and Loneliness**: Without face-to-face interactions, students may struggle with feelings of disconnection. In digital learning environments, where social interaction is more limited, students can experience increased feelings of loneliness and a reduced sense of belonging.

- **Communication gaps:** Tone and intent can be easily misunderstood in online discussions, which makes empathy and careful communication more important than ever.

- **Stress and overload:** With constant notifications, online assignments, and the blurred line between home and school life, students often feel overwhelmed. These pressures make emotional regulation and coping strategies especially important in digital classrooms.

All of these issues point us back to SEL. When educators incorporate emotional intelligence into digital classrooms, they can provide students with tools for managing stress, connecting with others in meaningful ways, and staying engaged in their learning.

There's another dimension to this: the workforce of tomorrow. Employers are increasingly vocal about the value of "soft skills", which include things like teamwork, adaptability, and emotional intelligence. The *World Economic Forum's Future of Jobs Report*[4] lists emotional intelligence, resilience, and leadership among the most in-demand skills for the coming decade (WEF, 2023). When educators bring SEL into digital spaces, they not only prepare students for school success but also equip them for life beyond school.

If we step back and think about the digital classroom experience from a student's perspective, the need for SEL becomes even clearer. Imagine being a middle schooler and navigating math lessons online. There's a chat box, a teacher's voice coming through the screen, maybe some icons or faces of classmates in little squares. It's easy to feel invisible or to wonder if your voice matters.

Now, add the pressure of grades, constant notifications from social apps, and the uncertainty of whether your Wi-Fi will hold steady until the end of class. For many students, this is their daily reality.

SEL gives students the confidence to navigate these challenges. It helps them recognize, "I'm feeling anxious right now because I'm worried about how I'll sound on camera," or "I need to take a break because I'm overwhelmed." These are

---

[4] **World Economic Forum.** (2023). *The Future of Jobs Report 2023*. Retrieved from https://www.weforum.org/publications/the-future-of-jobs-report-2023

not small things. In fact, they're the building blocks of resilience.

Developing emotional awareness and regulation supports students' ability to stay engaged, manage stress, and adapt effectively to the demands of online learning.

But SEL doesn't just benefit individual students; it strengthens entire learning communities. When classrooms, digital or physical, are built on empathy, respect, and collaboration, students feel safer taking risks and making mistakes. This sense of belonging is a powerful motivator.

According to Freeman et al. (2007)[5], a strong sense of classroom community has been linked to higher student engagement and persistence (*Journal of Experimental Education*). In digital classrooms, where distance can easily erode connection, these social bonds are especially vital.

Educators also benefit from integrating SEL. Teachers who intentionally nurture emotional intelligence often report stronger relationships with students and greater satisfaction in their work. Teaching can be emotionally demanding, and digital teaching brings its own set of challenges, from managing breakout rooms to monitoring online discussions. SEL practices offer teachers frameworks to stay grounded, manage stress, and model healthy emotional regulation for their students.

---

[5] **Freeman, T. M., Anderman, L. H., & Jensen, J. M.** (2007). *Sense of belonging in college freshmen at the classroom and campus levels. Journal of Experimental Education, 75*(3), 203–220. https://doi.org/10.3200/JEXE.75.3.203-220

All these points toward a larger truth: digital education without SEL risks becoming transactional, a matter of "deliver content, complete tasks, check boxes." But education at its best is transformational. It shapes not only what students know but also who they become. That is why SEL belongs at the heart of digital classrooms.

Objectives of the Book

This book was written with a very practical goal in mind: to help educators, school leaders, and communities bring SEL into digital learning in ways that are meaningful, sustainable, and impactful. To do that, we've organized the work around clear objectives that guide each chapter. Let's walk through them, not as abstract bullet points but as living questions to which we'll keep returning.

1. Understanding the Foundations of SEL

Before we can integrate SEL effectively, we need to understand what it is. SEL isn't just a buzzword; it's a research-based framework built on decades of study. We'll begin by unpacking the five core competencies — self-awareness, self-management, social awareness, relationship skills, and responsible decision-making — and explore how each plays out differently in digital contexts.

For example, what does self-management look like when students juggle multiple apps, assignments, and distractions at home? How do we teach empathy when interactions are mediated by screens? Grounding ourselves in the fundamentals ensures we move forward with clarity and purpose.

2. Exploring the Role of Technology

Technology is not neutral. It can either amplify connection or deepen disconnection. This book will look honestly at both sides. On one hand, digital tools can give students powerful ways to express themselves, collaborate across borders, and access resources that were unimaginable a generation ago.

On the other hand, they can introduce distractions, fuel comparison, and create barriers when access is unequal. We'll explore strategies to ensure technology supports SEL rather than undermining it.

For example, how can video conferencing tools be used to foster genuine dialogue? How can digital platforms be designed with inclusivity in mind? Research from the *Pew Research Center* shows that while technology can expand opportunities, disparities in access remain a significant equity issue (Vogels, E. A., 2021, June 22)[6]. Addressing this tension is central to our work.

3. Implementing Effective Strategies

Ideas only matter if they can be put into practice. That's why a major objective of this book is to provide concrete, evidence-based strategies for educators. We'll look at ways to

---

[6] Vogels, E. A. (2021, June 22). *Digital divide persists even as Americans with lower incomes make gains in tech adoption.* Pew Research Center.
https://www.pewresearch.org/short-reads/2021/06/22/digital-divide-persists-even-as-americans-with-lower-incomes-make-gains-in-tech-adoption/

integrate SEL seamlessly into daily routines, assignments, and classroom culture.

For instance, how might a teacher begin an online class with a quick emotional check-in that takes less than two minutes but sets the tone for the day? Or how can group projects in digital spaces be structured to build collaboration skills and empathy?

Research in *Child Development* confirms that SEL programs are most effective when they are integrated into the fabric of teaching, rather than added as an extra component (Durlak et al., 2011).

4. Engaging Families and Communities

SEL doesn't stop when the class ends or the device shuts down. Families and communities play an essential role in reinforcing the skills students practice at school. In digital education, where the line between home and school is blurred, it becomes even more important. We'll explore ways to partner with families, from simple communication strategies to more structured collaborations.

Community organizations can also be powerful allies, offering mentorship and real-world contexts for practicing social-emotional skills. Research has shown that when families are engaged, students demonstrate stronger academic achievement and better behavior (Henderson & Mapp, 2002)[7].

---

[7] Henderson, A. T., & Mapp, K. L. (2002). *A new wave of evidence: The impact of school, family, and community connections on student achievement* (PDF). SEDL. Retrieved from https://sedl.org/connections/resources/evidence.pdf

5. Assessing SEL

How do we know if SEL efforts are making a difference? Assessment can feel tricky because social and emotional skills often don't align with standardized tests. But that doesn't mean we can't measure growth. This book will highlight qualitative and quantitative approaches, including self-reflections, teacher observations, and well-designed surveys, that provide insight into students' development.

The goal is not to reduce emotions to numbers, but to use data as a guide for improvement. According to a framework by the *RAND Corporation*, thoughtful SEL assessments can help schools track progress, identify needs, and refine their practices (Hamilton et al., 2019)[8].

6. Preparing for the Future

Finally, this book looks ahead. Education is not static; it's constantly evolving in response to cultural, technological, and global shifts. Preparing for the future means asking: how will SEL need to adapt as artificial intelligence becomes part of classrooms?

What happens as virtual and augmented reality make learning more immersive? And how do we prepare students not just for today's challenges but for tomorrow's unknowns? Reports from the *OECD* stress that the future of education will increasingly demand adaptability, creativity, and emotional

---

[8] Taylor, J. J., & Hamilton, L. S. (2019, March 28). *How do you measure social and emotional learning?* RAND Corporation. Retrieved from https://www.rand.org/pubs/commentary/2019/03/how-do-you-measure-social-and-emotional-learning.html

intelligence (OECD, 2020)[9]. By anticipating these shifts, we can ensure that SEL remains relevant and powerful in the years to come.

Challenges and Opportunities in Current Educational Settings

As we step into the reality of digital classrooms, it's important to be honest about what's working and what still gets in the way. The shift to online learning has brought incredible possibilities. But it has also brought multiple hurdles that affect both teaching and learning. Looking at these side by side helps us see where SEL becomes not just helpful, but necessary.

Challenges

- **Digital distractions**. Anyone who has taught or studied online knows how easy it is to drift away. With multiple tabs open, constant notifications, and social media a click away, students are often pulled in many directions at once. Research shows that multitasking in digital environments can fragment attention, leaving students more stressed and less productive (Rosen, Carrier, & Cheever, 2013[10]).

---

[9] **OECD.** (n.d.). *Directorate for Education and Skills.* Retrieved from https://www.oecd.org/en/about/directorates/directorate-for-education-and-skills.html

[10] **Rosen, L. D., Carrier, L. M., & Cheever, N. A.** (2013). *Facebook and texting made me do it: Media-induced task-switching while studying. Computers in Human Behavior, 29*(3), 948-958. https://doi.org/10.1016/j.chb.2012.12.001

- **Lack of face-to-face interaction.** Even with cameras on, the "human energy" of a shared classroom is hard to replicate. Students may feel isolated, less seen, and less connected to their peers. That absence can impact their motivation and sense of belonging.

- **Emotional overload.** The constant connectivity of online learning brings new pressures. Between screen fatigue, assignment alerts, and performance expectations, students may feel overwhelmed. These challenges can contribute to stress, mental fatigue, and burnout, making it essential to build strategies that help students manage their workload and maintain balance.

- **Equity and access.** Not every student has a quiet space to work, reliable internet, or updated devices. This "digital divide" isn't just about technology; it translates directly into emotional strain and reduced engagement. For SEL to work in digital classrooms, we must first acknowledge and address these gaps.

Opportunities

- **Innovative learning experiences.** Digital tools can unlock creativity. Whether it's through multimedia projects, collaborative documents, or real-time polls, technology gives students new ways to express themselves and connect with content. SEL comes alive here when students feel safe experimenting and taking risks.

- **Personalized learning.** Online platforms allow for tailoring, such as adjusting the pace, style, and format of learning. When students see that their unique strengths and needs are recognized, their motivation and emotional engagement increase (Pane, Steiner, Baird, & Hamilton, 2017[11]).

- **Global connections.** A classroom can now stretch across time zones and cultures. Students can collaborate with peers around the world, building empathy, cultural awareness, and social skills that go far beyond their local community.

- **Data-driven insights.** Digital platforms collect information not just on academic progress, but also on patterns of engagement and participation. This data, used wisely, can help educators identify when students might be emotionally withdrawing and intervene early with support.

Conclusion

When we look at both the challenges and opportunities, one thing becomes clear: digital learning isn't going away. What matters is how we shape it. SEL provides us with the tools to humanize digital classrooms, creating spaces where students feel connected, capable, and cared for. It's not about replacing

---

[11] Pane, J. F., Steiner, E. D., Baird, M. D., Hamilton, L. S., & Pane, J. D. (2017). *Informing progress: Insights on personalized learning implementation and effects* (RAND Report No. RR-2042-BMGF). RAND Corporation. https://www.rand.org/pubs/research_reports/RR2042.html

technology with emotion, but about weaving them together so that learning feels both meaningful and sustainable.

This book is an invitation to educators, families, and communities to see SEL not as an "extra" but as the very foundation of digital learning. By building classrooms where students can thrive emotionally and academically, we're preparing them for not just tests or grades but for life.

Reflective Questions

1.   When you think about your own teaching or learning, which of the digital challenges listed here feels most familiar?

2.   How might SEL strategies help you address issues like distraction or emotional overload in your context?

3.   Which opportunities excite you most: personalization, global connections, or innovative tools? Why?

4.   How can you make sure equity stays central in your approach to digital SEL?

Chapter 2: The SEL Blueprint Foundations

Definition and Significance of SEL in Education

When discussing Social and Emotional Learning (SEL), we are not reaching for a buzzword. We are naming the everyday skills that let learning take hold: how we notice what we feel, how we manage that feeling, how we treat one another, and how we choose our next step with care.

These skills are not optional in a digital classroom—where we move between platforms, interpret messages without tone, and share space with home distractions. They are the conditions that make participation possible.

You already see this in small moments. A student pauses before typing and asks a clarifying question instead of assuming intent. Another uses a quiet reset to settle after a glitchy connection. A group decides how it will split the work rather than drifting into silence. None of this is flashy, and none of it requires a special program to begin. It requires clarity about what we are building and consistency in how we build it.

SEL gives us that clarity. It offers a shared language, allowing us to communicate with students—and with one another—about what helps learning feel steady and human. It also prompts us to consider climate: how safe it feels to speak, how predictable routines are, and how we respond when we misread each other online.

Good SEL is not just skill practice; it is a way of running a classroom so that belonging, voice, and dignity show up in daily routines. Field guides[12] that compare programs and practices say essentially the same thing: coherence matters more than volume. A few well-chosen routines, applied consistently, do more than long lists that come and go.

Another shift you will notice is the focus on identity, agency, and belonging. We cannot ask students to "self-regulate" in a space that does not recognize who they are or how they want to participate. If we want students to take risks, we have to show them that their voice will be met with respect and that they have real choices in how they engage.

This is not a soft add-on; it is how motivation and persistence grow. A contemporary strand of SEL work—often called "transformative SEL[13]"—makes this explicit and keeps us honest about equity as part of the core, not an afterthought.

In short, SEL helps us align our practices with what we already know to be true: we learn better when we feel seen, when expectations are clear, and when we have a way to recover together after mistakes. In digital classrooms, that

---

[12] Jones, S. M., Brush, K. E., Ramirez, T., Mao, Z. X., Marenus, M., Wettje, S., Finney, K., Raisch, N., Podoloff, N., Kahn, J., Barnes, S., Stickle, L., Brion-Meisels, G., McIntyre, J., Cuartas, J., & Bailey, R. (2021). *Navigating social and emotional learning from the inside out: Looking inside and across 33 leading SEL programs: A practical resource for schools and OST providers* (Revised and expanded 2nd ed.). Harvard Graduate School of Education. https://doi.org/10.59656/YD-OS5671.001

[13] Jagers, R. J., Rivas-Drake, D., & Williams, B. (2019). Transformative social and emotional learning (SEL): Toward SEL in service of educational equity and excellence. *Educational Psychologist, 54*(3), 162–184. https://doi.org/10.1080/00461520.2019.1623032

alignment is the difference between compliance and genuine engagement.

Overview of SEL Competencies

The most widely used SEL map organizes the work into five interconnected areas. You do not have to master a new vocabulary to use it, and you do not need a separate block in the timetable. What you need are a few routines that give each area a designated space in your class, whether you are in a room together or meeting through a screen.

1. Self-awareness

Self-awareness is the simple, steady practice of noticing: *What am I feeling? What is the story I'm telling myself? How is that story shaping what I do next?* In digital spaces, we lose many cues, so we rely even more on our inner read.

You and I can help students by normalizing quick check-ins that use plain language ("anxious," "frustrated," "ready," "distracted"), by inviting them to name one need ("I need a minute," "I need the instructions again"), and by showing that asking for support is part of how this class works.

Doing that regularly lowers the cost of participating and makes it easier for students to catch themselves before a small wobble becomes a spin.

2. Self-management

Self-management is regulation in motion. It is what allows a student to stay with a task when motivation dips or returns after an interruption without feeling ashamed. In online learning, where tabs compete for attention, we should not expect raw willpower to carry the day.

We can build the environment to help: short intervals with clear start and stop cues, timers that belong to the class (not just the teacher), visible lists that break a bigger task into a sequence, and predictable pauses to reset. When these rhythms are consistent, students practice regulation as part of the routine rather than treating it like a private struggle.

3. Social Awareness

Social awareness is perspective-taking and empathy. It shows up when we pause before reacting in a text thread. Remember that delay does not always mean disinterest, and choose language that leaves room for others. Because tone and body language travel poorly through chat, we teach students to ask more and assume less.

We also make our own intentions explicit ("I'm asking to understand, not to challenge") so students can model that clarity with one another. The result is not perfection, but fewer avoidable conflicts—and a shared way to repair when something goes wrong.

4. Relationship Skills

Relationship skills are the everyday moves that enable groups to work effectively: setting roles, checking for understanding, asking for help, and addressing friction without escalating it into a fight. In a digital project, clarity is kindness. We keep overhead low by agreeing on a small set of roles (for example, facilitator, timekeeper, scribe, checker), by documenting decisions where everyone can see them, and by deciding in advance how we will proceed if we disagree. None of this eliminates conflict; it simply provides a fair way to navigate it and return to work.

5. Responsible Decision-making

Responsible decision-making is how values turn into action. It is the habit of asking, *What are my options? What matters here— safety, accuracy, fairness, credit? What happens if I choose this path?* Digital learning adds layers: how we cite, how we protect privacy, what constitutes acceptable assistance, and how we demonstrate respect in public threads.

The more specific we are about what is allowed and why, the more students can develop ethical judgment without relying on guesswork. When we ask them to explain their reasoning, we also teach them that integrity is something we do, not just something we name.

These five areas support one another. Self-awareness and self-management help students meet the moment; social awareness and relationship skills help them meet one another; responsible decision-making brings both together so choices reflect care for self and community. Our job is not to cover everything at once. Our job is to pick a few repeatable practices and keep them steady enough that students can trust them.

The Impact of SEL on Academic Performance and Emotional Well-Being

We are not taking SEL on faith. There is a growing body of evidence—spanning international datasets, comparative guides, and studies of remote teaching—that points in the same direction: students and teachers do better when these skills are made visible and practiced on purpose.

Learning Behaviors and Achievement

Large-scale international reporting[14] connects specific social and emotional skills (responsibility, perseverance, self-control, curiosity) with academic outcomes for students at ages 10 and 15. These relationships persist even when background factors are considered. Our takeaway is practical: routines that help students plan, persist, and try again are not niceties; they are academic supports, especially when learning is blended or online.

Belonging and Engagement in Remote Teaching

When many schools shifted to remote formats, teachers reported exactly what you and I would expect: engagement dipped when connection thinned, misunderstandings multiplied in text-only channels, and the emotional load of constant adjustment was real. Research[15] that surveyed K–12

---

[14] OECD. (2024). *Social and emotional skills for better lives: Findings from the OECD Survey on Social and Emotional Skills 2023.* OECD Publishing. https://doi.org/10.1787/35ca7b7c-en

[15] Leech, N. L., Gullett, S., Cummings, M. H., & Haug, C. A. (2022). The challenges of remote K–12 education during the COVID-19 pandemic: Differences by grade level. *Online Learning, 26*(1), 245–267. https://doi.org/10.24059/olj.v26i1.2609

teachers during this period aligns with those observations and underlines our challenge: we have to build structures that protect inclusion, clarify expectations, and support calm attention. That is SEL, and it is buildable.

Self-assessment and Self-regulation

One of the most reliable ways to help students manage their learning is to explicitly teach self-assessment—how to compare current work to a clear standard, plan the next step, and monitor progress without waiting for the grade. A meta-analytic review[16] found positive effects of guided self-assessment on both self-regulated learning and self-efficacy.

In digital settings, we can tuck this into the flow of assignments with one or two short prompts at submission and simple progress trackers. The point is not to collect more data; the point is to help students understand their own process and make adjustments.

Identity, agency, and belonging are core, not extra

If we want students to bring their attention and effort, they need to see that their voice matters and that they have real choices in how to participate. This is the heart of transformative SEL: tying self- and social development to dignity, participation, and justice rather than reducing it to compliance.

---

[16] Andrade, H., & Valtcheva, A. (2009). Promoting learning and achievement through self-assessment. *Theory Into Practice, 48*(1), 12–19. https://doi.org/10.1080/00405840802577544

In digital classrooms, agency might manifest as choosing between a short audio reply and a written post, deciding whether a camera-on contribution or a thoughtful chat message best suits the moment, or proposing an alternative way to demonstrate understanding. When those options are genuine, students do not feel like guests in their own learning.

Program quality and coherence

Comparative guides that scan dozens of programs point toward the same design features: developmental fit, cultural responsiveness, explicit skill building, and integration with regular instruction. For us, that means selecting routines that can live inside the platforms we already use—our learning management system, discussion boards, and shared documents—so students encounter the same supportive moves across classes rather than a patchwork.

Integrating SEL into Digital Learning Environments

The strategies below keep your original intent and language, add warmth, and make each move concrete without turning it into a heavy lift. You can begin with one or two and build from there.

1. Leverage Technology for SEL

We do not need new tools; we need to use our current tools with purpose. A one-line emotion check-in at the start of a session ("choose a word that fits how you're arriving") gives us a quick read without forcing disclosure. A reflection box

attached to assignments ("What helped you stay engaged?")
turns SEL from a poster into a habit.

Shared planning docs with role fields make contributions
visible and fair. The test for any feature is simple: does it make
thinking, collaboration, or reflection easier to see and support?
If yes, keep it. If not, let it go.

2. Create Safe Online Spaces

Safety online is built on predictability and repair. We post
norms in plain language, revisit them briefly, and model what
happens when we misread each other. A class might agree that
in chat, we "assume positive intent, ask before judging, and
credit ideas by name." We might set response windows ("If
you post, expect a reply within 24 hours on school days") so
students do not wonder whether silence means disinterest.

Research from K–12 teachers during remote learning
highlights how much these small, steady moves matter for
engagement. They lower the emotional cost of showing up.

3. Incorporate Mindfulness Practices

We do not need long routines here. Thirty to sixty seconds
at a transition helps. We can invite a breath and then pair it
with action: "Type your next step in the chat." By making this
predictable, we help students reset without paying attention to
those who need it most.

4. Encourage Reflection and Self-assessment

Two short prompts at the end of a task are enough to build
the habit: "What did you do to manage distraction?" and

"What will you do first next time?" Over weeks, students learn to name their own helpful moves.

When we see a pattern, we adjust a routine and say so ("Many of us struggled to keep track of roles; next time we'll use a simple shared grid"). The research base behind guided self-assessment gives us confidence that this is not busywork; it is how self-regulation grows.

5. Promote Family Involvement

Families do not need a binder. They need quick, practical cues[17]. We can send a brief note explaining what we are practicing this month (for example, "asking for help at the right time" or "naming the next step"), what an adult at home might say in two minutes ("Tell me your plan for the first ten minutes"), and whom to contact for help. When families share what works for their child at home, we fold that into our routines. Small loops like this build trust.

6. Utilize Data for Continuous Improvement

Data for SEL should be light and formative. A two-item weekly pulse ("I felt heard this week: 1–5; One move I'll try next time: ____") can guide a single change in how we run the class. We share the pattern with students and explain what we will try. International reporting[18] on social and emotional skills

---

[17] Greenberg, M. T. (2023, March 6). *Evidence for social and emotional learning in schools*. Learning Policy Institute.
https://learningpolicyinstitute.org/product/evidence-social-emotional-learning-schools-brief

[18] Organisation for Economic Co-operation and Development. (2021). *OECD Survey on Social and Emotional Skills: Technical report*. OECD Publishing.

emphasizes this stance: use information to guide support, not to label students. That is how we protect dignity while improving the class climate.

7. Keep Equity Central

We cannot ask students to regulate away structural barriers. If bandwidth is thin, the device is shared, and the home space is noisy, we build flexible ways to participate that do not penalize those realities. That may mean accepting a written post when audio is unstable, giving wider windows for contributions, or providing alternative prompts when camera use is difficult.

The point is not to lower expectations; it is to make meeting them possible. This is where identity, agency, and belonging move from talk to practice[19].

What the Evidence Means for Your Classroom

Rather than theory for its own sake, the research points us to a handful of practical truths. You can use these as anchors as you plan.

- **Attention and persistence improve** when students have routines for planning and for resetting after interruptions—both frequent needs in digital learning.

---

https://www.oecd.org/content/dam/oecd/en/about/programmes/edu/survey-on-social-and-emotional-skills/Technical%20Report%20SSES.pdf

[19] Jagers, R. J., Skoog-Hoffman, A., Barthelus, B., & Schlund, J. (2021, Summer). Transformative social emotional learning: In pursuit of educational equity and excellence. *American Educator, 45*(2), 12–17, 39. https://eric.ed.gov/?id=EJ1304336

International results connect these skills with achievement across ages and contexts.

- **Engagement and belonging rise** when norms are predictable and repair is modeled. This was one of the strongest themes in teachers' accounts of remote teaching.

- **Confidence grows** when self-assessment is taught rather than assumed. Students become more accurate judges of their work and more willing to try again.

- **Equity is protected** when SEL includes identity and agency, not just compliance. Students participate more when they have meaningful options in how they contribute.

- **Coherence beats volume.** Program guides favor approaches that fit the context, build explicit skills, and live inside everyday instruction. That is the path we'll take through the rest of this book.

Conclusion

If Chapter 1 sets the purpose, this chapter gives us a map. We are choosing to build classrooms—physical and digital—that feel clear, humane, and durable. We will use the SEL competencies not as a separate agenda but as a vocabulary for our everyday decisions: how we start and end, how we invite and respond, how we ask for help, and how we repair.

We will keep the work small enough to be consistent and wide enough to include every student. We will measure our success not only by grades or completion rates but also by whether students feel they belong, can steady themselves when it is hard, and can treat others with care while doing demanding work.

In the chapters ahead, we will move from definitions to practice: the routines that anchor self-awareness and self-management, the norms that protect inclusion in chat and on video, and the choices that make decision-making ethical in digital spaces. We will start where we are, take one or two steps, and keep going together.

Reflection Questions

1. Where could a 30-60 second reset naturally fit in your current lesson flow, and what would you pair it with so it leads to action (e.g., "type your next step")?

2. Which single norm would most reduce the emotional cost of participating in your class (tone, timing, credit), and how will you make it visible?

3. Which two self-assessment prompts would help your students plan their next step without adding to the grading load?

4. What is one participation option you can offer (audio vs. text; camera vs. chat) that preserves rigor while honoring different contexts?

Discussion Questions

- How will we coordinate small shared routines across courses so students do not relearn expectations every period? What two will we start with?

- How will we know if students feel heard in our digital spaces, and what change will we make if the answer is "not enough"?

One Practical Activity (Simple, Repeatable)

Two-Item End-of-Task Self-Check (2 minutes).

Add to every digital submission:

1. "Name one move you used to manage focus or collaboration today."

2. "What is your next step, and what do you need for it?" Review patterns weekly and adjust one routine in response. This applies the evidence on guided self-assessment to the work students are already doing.

Chapter 3: Building a Positive Classroom Culture Online

Introduction

Creating a positive classroom culture is vital for student engagement, motivation[20], and emotional well-being[21], especially in digital learning environments. While traditional classrooms provide physical spaces for interaction, digital classrooms require intentional strategies to cultivate a sense of community and belonging[22].

In this chapter, we will explore the significance of building a positive online classroom culture, share anecdotes and quotes from students about their experiences, provide detailed strategies for fostering community, and address potential challenges along with practical solutions.

A healthy online culture is built from small, steady moves we repeat: clear norms, predictable routines, and tools used with purpose rather than noise—choices that research on online learning has linked to more effective participation and overall learning outcomes.

---

[20] Reeve, J., & Cheon, S. H. (2021). Autonomy-supportive teaching: Its malleability, benefits, and potential to improve educational practice. Educational Psychologist, 56(1), 54–77. https://doi.org/10.1080/00461520.2020.1862657

[21] Wilkins, N. J., Krause, K. H., Verlenden, J. V., Szucs, L. E., Blob, C., Lee, S. M., … & Underwood, J. M. (2023). School connectedness and risk behaviors and experiences among high school students — Youth Risk Behavior Survey, United States, 2021. *MMWR Supplements, 72*(Suppl-1), 13–21. https://doi.org/10.15585/mmwr.su7201a

[22] Walton, G. M., & Cohen, G. L. (2011, March 17). *A brief social-belonging intervention improves academic and health outcomes of minority students* [PDF]. Retrieved from https://orsl.usc.edu/wp-content/uploads/2022/10/Walton-Cohen_2011-belonging-intervention.pdf

When students feel connected to the people and purpose of a class, they're more likely to show up, contribute, and persist; national monitoring reports also associate school connectedness [23]with better mental-health indicators and academic outcomes.

The online medium changes how we notice and respond to one another, but it doesn't change what we need: a community where we're known by name, where expectations are visible, and where there's a fair way to repair when messages land wrong.

You and I can help that culture take root by naming what matters (respect, credit for ideas, timely replies), inviting voice in low-pressure ways, and designing participation so every student has a way in—camera, chat, audio, or a quick post. Done consistently, these moves make it easier for students to take academic risks and to re-enter the work after an interruption, which supports engagement and motivation without adding extra weight to your day.

The Importance of Positive Classroom Culture

A positive classroom culture lays the foundation for effective learning. When we talk about culture, we mean the everyday feel of the space: how we greet one another, how we

---

[23] Sliwa, S. A., Merlo, C. L., McKinnon, I. I., Self, J. L., Kissler, C. J., Saelee, R., & Rasberry, C. N. (2024). *Skipping breakfast and academic grades, persistent feelings of sadness or hopelessness, and school connectedness among high school students — Youth Risk Behavior Survey, United States, 2023* (MMWR Suppl 73, Suppl-4, 87–93). https://www.cdc.gov/mmwr/volumes/73/su/pdfs/su7304a10-H.pdf

handle mistakes, and how predictable the experience is from day to day.

Research describes this as the school/classroom climate—the norms, relationships, safety, and structures that shape how learning actually occurs. In digital settings, where hallway conversations and subtle nonverbal cues are absent, this climate is intentionally built: it is characterized by clear expectations, fair processes, and visible care.

Culture shows up first in relationships. When students experience steady teacher support, they engage more, behave better, and learn more. A large meta-analysis documents significant links between teacher–student relationship quality and both engagement and achievement[24], underscoring that how we relate is not separate from what students achieve.

That's even more true online, where warmth and clarity have to travel through text, audio, and video. When we make time to greet by name, credit ideas in chat, and respond within predictable windows, we're not only being kind; we're building the conditions for participation.

A second pillar is belonging—that everyday sense that "people like me learn here." Small design choices matter: explicit norms that signal respect, options for how to contribute (voice, chat, brief posts), and feedback that recognizes effort and strategy. In online courses, making people feel "real and reachable" to one another—often called

---

[24] Roorda, D. L., Jak, S., Zee, M., & Oort, F. J. (2017). *Affective teacher–student relationships and students' engagement and achievement: A meta-analytic update and test of the mediating role of engagement.* Social Psychology of Education, 20(3), 585–610. https://doi.org/10.17105/SPR-2017-0035.V46-3

social presence—is consistently associated with better course satisfaction and perceived learning. When we help students feel seen and heard, they stay with us longer—through glitches, through challenging tasks, and through the quiet moments that can otherwise drift.

Positive culture also supports motivation. Students are more willing to take academic risks when they experience autonomy (genuine choices), competence (clear goals and scaffolded steps), and relatedness (trusting connections). In online contexts, course studies report higher engagement when we design for active interaction and timely presence[25]: timely replies, opportunities to collaborate, and tasks that ask students to do something with what they're learning. None of this requires fancy tools; it requires clarity about how we'll work together and consistency in sticking to it.

We also see culture in behavior—not as compliance for its own sake, but as collective habits that make learning possible. Reviews of climate research link positive classroom climates with fewer conduct issues, better attendance, and stronger academic outcomes across grade levels (literature summary)[26]. Online, the same logic holds: if norms are plain, roles are fair, and repair is expected when messages land poorly, we spend less time firefighting and more time learning.

---

[25] Martin, F., & Bolliger, D. U. (2018, March). *Engagement matters: Student perceptions on the importance of engagement strategies in the online learning environment. Online Learning, 22*(1), 205–222. https://files.eric.ed.gov/fulltext/EJ1179659.pdf

[26] Aspen Institute. (2020, August). *School climate literature review* [PDF].https://www.aspeninstitute.org/wp-content/uploads/2020/08/Aspen-Institute-School-Climate-Literature-Review.pdf

In digital environments, the structure of the experience does a lot of heavy lifting. Studies in online learning show that clear organization, transparent criteria, and regular, meaningful interaction predict stronger engagement and performance.

Course-level work has found that clarity of structure and instructor presence relate to students' satisfaction and persistence. That translates into a few simple moves we can repeat: opening routines that orient students, short work blocks with visible goals, and closing prompts that help students identify their next step.

Culture matters for equity as well. A physical or digital classroom can only feel safe if every student has a workable way to participate. Approaches like Universal Design for Learning[27] remind us to provide multiple means of engagement and expression.

This can involve accepting text or audio responses, keeping camera use optional when bandwidth or privacy is a concern, or offering multiple routes to demonstrate understanding. These adjustments don't lower expectations; they remove unnecessary barriers, making expectations more reachable.

Trust is a powerful—often invisible—part of culture. When trust is high, students are more likely to ask for help, admit confusion, and stay engaged through difficulty. Longitudinal work in schools shows that relational trust among students and

---

[27] CAST. (2024). *Universal Design for Learning Guidelines version 3.0*. Retrieved from https://udlguidelines.cast.org

educators is associated with improved learning conditions and outcomes (Trust in Schools[28]).

We build that trust online the same way we do in person: by keeping promises about timing, giving credit reliably, and repairing when we miss the mark.

Put together, the case is straightforward. Positive culture isn't a poster or a paragraph in a syllabus; it's the daily pattern students can count on. Online, we don't rely on the room to do the work for us—we design the room. When we center relationships, belonging, structure, equity, trust, and care, we create the conditions where engagement, motivation, and well-being have room to grow.

Anecdotes and Quotes from Students

1. Sense of Belonging

"At first, I felt like I was just another face on the screen, but our teacher really made an effort to get to know us. She started each class with a fun question, and it helped me feel like I belonged to a community." – Sarah, 10th Grade

Belonging grows from steady, predictable signals: we use names, invite low-pressure check-ins, and make room for brief personal details that help us see one another. Those small moves matter. Classic research[29] on the psychological sense of

---

[28] Schneider, B. (2003, March 1). *Trust in schools: A core resource for school reform.* ASCD. https://www.ascd.org/el/articles/trust-in-schools-a-core-resource-for-school-reform

[29] Goodenow, C. (1993). *The psychological sense of school membership among adolescents: Scale development and educational correlates* [PDF].

school membership shows that when students feel respected and included, they report higher motivation, effort, and achievement—especially in adolescence. Turn this into practice by keeping a standing opener (one question, one round), crediting ideas by name in chat, and making sure every student has at least one safe way to contribute (voice, chat, or a quick post).

2. Supportive Interactions

"During group projects, I felt nervous about sharing my ideas. But my classmates were so supportive. They always encouraged me, and it made me more confident in speaking up." – Jamal, 9th Grade

Support doesn't appear by accident online; we design for it. Giving roles (facilitator, timekeeper, summarizer), norms for turn-taking, and a simple "credit what you build on" line can lower the cost of speaking up.

Research[30] on peer-assisted learning in online formats documents how structured peer roles and encouragement increase participation and confidence, particularly when the routines are clear and repeatable. A quick way to start: post the roles in a shared doc each time, rotate them, and add a one-line debrief ("What helped our talk stay fair today?").

---

https://bibliotecadigital.mineduc.cl/bitstream/handle/20.500.12365/17469/good enow1993.pdf

[30] Rawson, R., & Rhodes, C. (2022). *Peer-Assisted Learning Online: Peer Leader Motivations and Experiences.* Journal of Peer Learning, 15, 32–47. https://journalofpeerlearning.org/articles/105/files/66951d90e5743.pdf

A second piece here is psychological safety[31]—the permission to ask questions and risk ideas without embarrassment. When safety is high, students engage longer and more deeply in instructional activities; analyses in online and blended contexts find increased participation when norms for respectful listening and error-friendly talk are explicit. Two fast moves: normalize "I'm not sure yet" as an acceptable response and model graceful repair when a comment lands wrong.

3. A Safe Space for Expression

"Our teacher created a space where we could talk about our feelings, especially during tough times like exams. It felt good to know that we could share our worries and not be judged." – Emily, 11th Grade

A "safe space" online is practical, not abstract. We can schedule a one-minute reset at transitions, keep an "I need a minute" option visible (e.g., an emoji or quick chat code), and offer short regulation choices that students can use without being singled out.

Implementation guidance on calming and choice-based practices[32] shows that predictable, in-the-moment regulation options help students de-stress and return to the task without derailing instruction (open PDF: WestEd brief, 2022). If

---

[31] Tu, X. (2021). *The role of classroom culture and psychological safety in EFL students' engagement. Frontiers in Psychology, 12*, Article 760903. https://doi.org/10.3389/fpsyg.2021.760903

[32] Buckner, L. (2022). *Calming spaces in schools and classrooms* [PDF]. WestEd for California Safe & Supportive Schools. https://ca-safe-supportive-schools.wested.org/wp-content/uploads/2022/10/Calming-Spaces-in-Schools-and-Classrooms.pdf

bandwidth or privacy is an issue, allow students to type their choice or use a reaction icon rather than speaking.

4. Feeling Seen by the Teacher

"It mattered that our teacher said my name in chat and noticed when I'd been quiet. It made me want to come back the next day." – Luis, 8th Grade

Being "seen" is the day-to-day face of teacher presence: quick name-use, timely feedback, and noticing when a usually active student goes quiet. Recent qualitative research[33] with high-school online teachers describes the small, replicable moves that signal presence—paralinguistic cues, warm tone in written announcements, and individualized check-ins—paired with rationales teachers use to prioritize them.

Two habits to try: a standing 24-hour reply window on school days and a short weekly "I notice…" message that acknowledges specific effort or progress.

These anecdotes demonstrate that when educators prioritize building a positive online classroom culture, students feel more connected, supported, and engaged in their learning experiences.

---

[33] Bowden, M. R., & Moore, J. A. (2025). *Cue the paralinguistics: A qualitative case study of teacher social presence* [PDF]. *Journal of Online Learning Research, 11*(2), 169–185. https://files.eric.ed.gov/fulltext/EJ1481634.pdf

Strategies for Fostering a Sense of Community in Digital Classrooms

1. Establish Clear Expectations and Norms

A strong online community starts with shared agreements we can all see and use. When we co-create simple norms with students, we replace guesswork with clarity and lower the emotional cost of joining in. Begin by asking, "What helps you participate without stress?" and "What makes discussion feel fair?"

Shape the responses into a short class agreement written in plain language. Keep it visible—pin it in the LMS, place it on the opening slide of live sessions, and refer to it briefly at the end: "Which norm helped us today?" Returning to the agreement signals that we mean what we say and that students have a voice in how the class runs.

Example: At the start of the year, lead a conversation about respect and kindness in online interactions. Students offer ideas, and you turn them into a social contract everyone can read and reference.

2. Encourage Regular Check-ins

Quick check-ins make the class feel human and give us a read on the room without taking over instruction. A one-minute opener—optional and low-pressure—helps students arrive, feel noticed, and set a plan.

Rotate simple prompts: a single word for how we arrive, a mood slider, or a private note if someone prefers not to publicly share. Follow with a plan question like, "What's your first step today?" We're not asking for deep disclosure; we're creating a predictable moment that says, "You matter here," and guiding attention toward the work.

Example: Start each class with a 1–5 mood check and offer anyone who wishes to share a sentence about why. Keep it light, keep it brief, and move smoothly into the day's task.

3. Create Opportunities for Collaboration

Community grows when students solve real tasks together. In digital spaces, clarity is kindness: short timelines, clear goals, and named roles bring more voices in. Use small groups and keep roles simple—facilitator, timekeeper, summarizer, checker—so everyone knows how to contribute.

Give each group one shared space to record decisions and next steps. Add a decision rule for stalemates ("If we're stuck after five minutes, we vote or test the smallest option"). Collaboration feels safe when expectations are clear and responsibilities are fair.

Example: Assign small groups to research a topic and present findings. Encourage shared documents for notes, a quick plan for who does what, and a brief check-in halfway through to keep progress visible.

4. Incorporate Icebreakers and Team-Building Activities

A little structured connection helps students feel comfortable speaking up, especially at the start of a course or a unit. Keep icebreakers short, relevant, and respectful of different comfort levels. Tie prompts to the learning when possible and set tight time boxes so the activity feels purposeful, not filler. Offer multiple ways to participate—voice, chat, or a quick post—so students can choose what works for them. The aim is not entertainment; it's trust and ease.

Example: Run a virtual scavenger hunt where students find and share an item from home that represents an interest or hobby. Keep it fast and friendly, and invite chat contributions for those who prefer typing.

5. Utilize Digital Storytelling

Digital storytelling lets students share identity, process, and growth in formats that make sense online. A focused prompt and clear length limit keep the task manageable and reduce performance pressure.

Offer choice in how to create—short video, audio over slides, comic strip, or illustrated post—and provide a simple structure (set-up, moment, takeaway). Share first in small groups to build confidence, then curate class highlights so the community can celebrate one another's voices and effort.

Example: Ask students to create a short video or presentation telling a personal story connected to the course—what challenged them, what helped them persist, or how their thinking shifted. Share in class with a few positive responses per story.

6. Celebrate Achievements and Milestones

Recognition makes effort visible and strengthens the sense that we're in this together. Celebrate the process as much as the product: ask for help at the right time, invite a quieter voice, revise after feedback, or persevere through a tough step. Keep celebrations frequent and light—shout-outs in chat, a "wins" slide, a quick note naming a specific move you noticed. This steady attention to growth builds motivation without turning praise into a performance.

Example: Host a brief end-of-month celebration where students share a success—completing a challenging assignment, reaching a personal goal, or helping a peer. Keep it upbeat and student-centered.

7. Provide Opportunities for Peer Feedback

Thoughtful peer feedback builds community and improves work at the same time. Use a simple, kind protocol so students know how to respond: "What's working?" and "One suggestion."

Ask them to point to something specific (a sentence, a figure, a step) so comments are grounded and useful. Close the loop by having each student name one next step they'll try based on the feedback. Over time, this becomes a routine that strengthens trust and skill.

Example: After a project, students exchange work in small groups and offer feedback using your two prompts. They then post a short note describing the change they plan to make before final submission.

8. Create a Digital Classroom Space for Social Interaction

Not every meaningful connection is academic. A low-stakes social space can reduce isolation and make it easier to speak up when the work gets demanding.

Set up one thread or channel for informal sharing—study playlists, book or movie recommendations, quick photos of study spaces. Keep the same guardrails you use in class, and remind students how to flag concerns. Seed the space with a weekly prompt, then step back and let students guide the conversation.

Example: Create a dedicated channel in your platform for hobby and media recommendations. Encourage students to post when they have time, respond to one another, and keep the tone welcoming.

These eight moves don't require new tools or long prep. They require consistency, clarity, and a willingness to let students help shape the space. When we keep them steady, our online classrooms feel more like communities—and students are more willing to show up, try, and keep going.

Potential Challenges and Solutions for Creating a Positive Culture Online

Digital classrooms invite rich connection, but they also surface predictable frictions. Naming those frictions—and planning calm, consistent responses—helps us preserve a culture where students can learn with confidence. The challenges below appear in most online settings; the accompanying practices keep the room humane, structured, and fair.

1. Feelings of Isolation

What we notice: Students attend but remain quiet, cameras are off by preference or circumstance, and participation is limited to a small core. The course begins to feel transactional.

Why it happens: Online spaces strip away many of the informal cues that help belonging grow—passing conversations, quick smiles, shared table work. Some students also face constraints at home that make on-mic or on-camera participation difficult.

What helps: Stability and invitation. Small, consistent routines—brief check-ins, name use in greetings, predictable opportunities to contribute by voice, chat, or short posts—signal that every student has a workable way in.

Keeping groups stable for a period of weeks allows relationships to form naturally; rotating simple roles (facilitator, timekeeper, summarizer, checker) distributes responsibility and draws in quieter classmates.

When a usually active student goes quiet, a private, respectful message ("I missed your voice today—anything I can adjust to make it easier to join next time?") restores connection without pressure.

2. Lack of Engagement

What we notice: Tasks are completed quickly and superficially; questions default to "Is this graded?"; discussions stall; submissions arrive without evidence of revision.

Why it happens: Engagement drops when a task's purpose is unclear, steps feel confusing or overly numerous, or when students cannot see how their effort leads to progress. Long stretches of independent work without visible milestones compound the problem.

What helps: Clarity and momentum. Each activity benefits from one explicit purpose, one visible product, and a sensible audience. Breaking larger assignments into short, timed work blocks with concrete interim deliverables keeps attention anchored. Limited and genuine choice (for example, voice, chat, or brief written post; slide deck or one-page explainer) allows students to match the task to their strengths without lowering expectations.

Quick formative moments—sharing a draft sentence, posting one example, or identifying a first next step—make thinking visible and keep the feedback loop short. Recognition of process ("You paused for clarification before starting— that's strong judgment") sustains effort even when the final product is still forming.

3. Miscommunication and Conflict

What we notice: Tone is misread in text threads; comments escalate quickly; a single misunderstanding silences participation for the rest of the session.

Why it happens: Without nonverbal cues, speed overtakes care. Students may not have language for disagreement, and the class may lack a shared path to repair when something lands poorly.

What helps: Shared language and deliberate pacing. Establish concise communication norms in plain language ("We challenge ideas, not people"; "Ask before judging") and teach a simple sequence for clarification and repair: ask to check understanding, restate what was heard, invite correction, then respond.

When a thread heats up, slow the tempo—pause for thirty seconds and ask everyone to draft before posting. Model the repair process yourself ("I misread your point; here's my rephrase") so students see that course culture makes room for correction without embarrassment.

For more serious missteps, follow up privately, name the impact and the expectation, and invite the student back in with dignity.

4. Digital Distractions

What we notice: Students drift during longer segments, tab back late from breaks, or struggle to re-enter the task after interruptions at home.

Why it happens: Online environments compete for attention. When activities lack clear milestones or when there is no shared cadence for work and pause, willpower alone is not enough to maintain focus—especially for learners juggling family responsibilities or unstable connectivity.

What helps: A shared rhythm. Work in short intervals (eight to twelve minutes) with one specific mini-deliverable, then a brief reset. Use a visible countdown or time calls so everyone works to the same clock. Before each interval, ask students to name their first move ("open the document," "label the diagram," "write the claim"); that single action lowers the barrier to starting.

After a reset, a three-word status in chat ("halfway—need example") helps students re-enter the lane. Offer light environmental suggestions (full-screen view, notifications off) as options, not requirements, so students who cannot change their settings are not penalized.

5. Cultural Differences and Inclusion

What we notice: A few voices dominate while others opt out; humor or idioms exclude; expectations for discussion feel unfamiliar to some students; participation appears uneven.

Why it happens: Students bring different discourse norms, levels of comfort with public speaking, and home circumstances that shape how they can be present online. "The usual way" of contributing often reflects a narrow set of preferences.

What helps: Multiple participation methods and norms that translate values into actions. Co-create a brief class agreement and define behaviors that express those values (credit ideas by name; invite a new voice before speaking again; ask before judging).

Offer more than one participation pathway—voice, chat, short posts, or audio notes—and keep camera use optional where bandwidth or privacy is a concern. Rotate roles so contribution is not measured by airtime alone; synthesizing, checking details, and documenting decisions are equally valued. Keep language accessible: avoid unexplained jargon, maintain a living glossary for course terms, and model how to request clarification without stigma.

Ensure examples and references reflect varied cultures and experiences so more students can see themselves in the work.

None of these practices is complicated; their strength lies in steadiness. When expectations are clear, roles are fair, communication has a clear path to resolution, and participation is possible in more than one way, students learn that your online classroom is a reliable place to think, try, and try again. That reliability, more than any single activity, is what protects a positive culture when the learning gets hard.

Conclusion

A positive online classroom grows from steady choices we make every day: clear norms, fair roles, predictable rhythms, and a simple way to repair misunderstandings. When we keep those choices visible and consistent, students experience the course as a community—not just a list of tasks.

This fits the Community of Inquiry[34] view that teaching, social, and cognitive presence work together to support meaningful learning. Choose one or two routines, invite students to shape them, and adjust based on what you notice. In digital spaces, steadiness builds trust—and trust makes learning durable.

Reflection Questions

- When did you feel most included in our online class this week?

---

[34] Athabasca University. (n.d.). *CoI framework*. Retrieved from https://coi.athabascau.ca/coi-model

- Which class norm helped you participate today?

- What is one change (by you or by us) that would make it easier to contribute next time?

- Where did you see a repair—someone clarifying or rephrasing—and what difference did it make?

Discussion Prompts (For a Staff Meeting)

- Where are our routines already clear, fair, and predictable—and where are they still vague?

- Which participation options (voice, chat, short post, audio note) are working for our learners? What else should we add?

- How will we check culture lightly each week (two quick questions) and show students what we changed based on their feedback?

Chapter 4: Understanding Emotions in a Digital Context

Introduction

In today's classrooms, learning often happens through windows and microphones rather than shared tables and hallways. That shift doesn't make emotions less present; it simply makes them easier to overlook. Students arrive carrying the same mix of curiosity, stress, pride, frustration, and hope they bring to any learning space—only now those feelings travel through chat boxes, icons, and brief camera moments.

When we make room for emotions in digital settings, two positive things happen: students feel steadier and more connected, and the work itself becomes easier to engage with and stay focused on.

This chapter examines emotional literacy in plain terms, how digital communication can influence relationships in either helpful or unhelpful ways, and provides a set of practical exercises that can be easily integrated into the class flow with minimal preparation.

Our aim is simple: to give students language for what they feel, provide them with safe ways to express it, and establish small routines that help them move from feeling to action. When those pieces are in place, online learning feels less like a list of tasks and more like a community where thinking and care can coexist.

The Importance of Emotional Literacy in Education

Emotional literacy is the ability to recognize, understand, and express emotions so that they support learning and relationships rather than derail them.

In a digital classroom, that might look like a student typing "I'm stuck—can I get the first step again?" instead of going silent, or taking a 60-second reset after a tech glitch before rejoining the group. These are small moves, but they protect attention and help the class move forward together.

Emotional literacy spans several connected skills:

- **Self-awareness:** naming what you're feeling and how it's shaping your focus.

- **Self-management:** choosing a steadying strategy— breathing, planning the first step, asking for help, or taking a short break.

- **Social awareness:** reading others' perspectives and experiences with care, especially when tone and body language travel poorly online.

- **Relationship skills:** communicating clearly, listening actively, repairing misreads, and collaborating fairly.

- **Ethical decision-making:** acting in ways that protect safety, dignity, and integrity in shared digital spaces.

Below are three through lines that link emotional literacy to school outcomes without turning the class into group therapy.

1. Research on Emotional Literacy and School Outcomes

A steady body of work shows that systematically teaching emotion skills can improve classroom climate and support learning. For example, research[35] connected to the Yale Center for Emotional Intelligence reports improvements in school climate, teacher well-being, and student outcomes when emotion skills are taught explicitly and reinforced in daily routines.

A complementary experimental thread—affect labeling[36]—finds that putting feelings into words can, in some contexts, ease reactivity and help people regain cognitive control, with classic studies showing decreased amygdala activity when emotions are labeled. Classroom translation: students don't need a long share; a single word or emoji paired with a plan is often enough to steady attention.

2. Emotional Literacy and Academic Success

Students who can identify what they feel and choose a next step tend to start sooner, persist longer, and ask for clarification earlier—habits that cushion grades and protect confidence.

Short routines make this practical: a two-question exit ticket ("What helped you persist today?" "What will you try first next

---

[35] Yale Center for Emotional Intelligence. (2019, April). *RULER: An evidence-based approach to social and emotional learning* [Brochure].
https://rulerapproach.org/wp-content/uploads/2019/04/RULER_Brochure.pdf

[36] Lieberman, M. D., Eisenberger, N. I., Crockett, M. J., Tom, S. M., Pfeifer, J. H., & Way, B. M. (2007). *Putting feelings into words: Affect labeling disrupts amygdala activity in response to affective stimuli. Psychological Science, 18*(5), 421–428.
https://doi.org/10.1111/j.1467-9280.2007.01916.x

time?") keeps emotion connected to action. When we notice and name specific process moves—pausing to clarify, inviting a quieter voice, revising after feedback—we reinforce the very behaviors that make challenging work possible.

3. Emotional Literacy and Mental Health

When emotions have a safe place to land, stress doesn't have to turn into shutdown. Brief, predictable mindfulness practices—used as part of class transitions—can help.

A recent systematic review[37] of school-based mindfulness interventions reports small-to-moderate benefits for stress and internalizing symptoms, with the strongest results when practices are short and regular. Our goal isn't to "fix" feelings; it's to give students a few reliable tools so they can return to thinking when the moment is turbulent.

The Impact of Digital Communication on Student Relationships

Technology changes how we read one another. In a classroom, quick glances and small smiles do a lot of social work. We rely on text, timing, and small symbols to carry tone online. That can be freeing—some students find it easier to speak up in chat than in a crowded room—but it can also invite misreads. Four patterns show up often.

---

[37] Phan, M. L., Renshaw, T. L., Caramanico, J., Greeson, J. M., MacKenzie, E., Atkinson-Diaz, Z., Doppelt, N., Tai, H., Mandell, D. S., & Nuske, H. J. (2022). *Mindfulness-based school interventions: A systematic review of outcome evidence quality by study design. Mindfulness, 13*(7), 1591–1613. https://doi.org/10.1007/s12671-022-01885-9

1. The Nature of Digital Communication

Without voice and body language, messages are easy to misunderstand. Classic experiments[38] show that people routinely overestimate how clearly their tone comes through in email; sarcasm and humor are particularly likely to be missed. In class, we can reduce friction by making intentions explicit ("I'm asking to understand, not to challenge") and by teaching a short repair script when something lands poorly.

2. Social Media and Emotional Dynamics

Social media can broaden connection and expression, but it can also magnify comparison, fear of missing out, and exposure to harm. The American Psychological Association's health advisory[39] urges adults to treat adolescent social media use as having mixed benefits alongside risks and to pair access with skill-building and context-aware boundaries.

The U.S. Surgeon General's advisory[40] similarly calls for shared responsibility among platforms, policymakers, schools, and families while evidence continues to develop. For our purposes, this means modeling balanced talk about online life and giving students language to notice when a feed is helping or harming their mood.

---

[38] Kruger, J., Epley, N., Parker, J., & Ng, Z. W. (2005). *Egocentrism over e-mail: Can people communicate as well as they think? Journal of Personality and Social Psychology, 89*(6), 925-936. https://web-docs.stern.nyu.edu/pa/kruger_email_ego.pdf

[39] American Psychological Association. (2023, May). *Health advisory on social media use in adolescence* [PDF]. Retrieved from https://www.apa.org/topics/social-media-internet/health-advisory-adolescent-social-media-use.pdf

[40] U.S. Department of Health and Human Services. (2023, May 23). *Social Media and Youth Mental Health: The U.S. Surgeon General's Advisory* [PDF]. Retrieved from https://www.hhs.gov/sites/default/files/sg-youth-mental-health-social-media-advisory.pdf

Recent polling adds context: a 2025 Pew Research Center report[41] found that nearly half of U.S. teens say they spend "too much time" on social media, with teen girls more likely than boys to report negative effects on mental health and sleep. Data like this doesn't tell us what any one student feels, but it reminds us to keep check-ins light, optional, and regular so students can ask for adjustments when they need them.

3. Cyberbullying and Its Effects

Distance and anonymity can license unkindness. Reviews[42] link cyberbullying victimization with higher depression, anxiety, and loneliness among adolescents. Ongoing surveys from the [43]Cyberbullying Research Center estimate that roughly a quarter to a third of teens report being cyberbullied in the last month, depending on the sample and measure.

In class, a posted norm set, swift private follow-ups, and clear support pathways help students trust that harm will be addressed and that everyone will be welcomed back with dignity.

---

[41] Faverio, M., Anderson, M., & Park, E. (2025, April 22). *Teens, social media and mental health.* Pew Research Center.
https://www.pewresearch.org/internet/2025/04/22/teens-social-media-and-mental-health/
[42] Nixon, C. L. (2014). *Current perspectives: The impact of cyberbullying on adolescent health.* Adolescent Health, Medicine and Therapeutics, 5, 143-158.
https://doi.org/10.2147/AHMT.S36456
https://www.ncbi.nlm.nih.gov/pmc/articles/PMC4126576/
[43] Patchin, J. W., & Hinduja, S. (2024). *2023 Cyberbullying Data.* Cyberbullying Research Center. Retrieved October 20, 2025, from
https://cyberbullying.org/2023-cyberbullying-data

4. Building Positive Relationships Online

Digital tools can also strengthen connections when we use them with intention. Small signals matter: simple acknowledgment, crediting ideas by name, and shared role structures all widen participation.

There's even evidence[44] that emoticons and emojis, used thoughtfully, can increase the sense that people are "real and reachable" in text-based settings. For us, that translates into a few predictable conventions—what emoji signals "ready," how to ask for clarification, and how we repair—and then modeling them until they become second nature.

Practical Exercises for Implementing Emotional Awareness Activities

Your original list of ten activities follows, rewritten in a warm, steady tone and expanded so they're easy to run online. Keep them light. Choose a few that fit your context and repeat them often enough that students can trust the pattern.

1. Emotion Journals

Description: Students keep a private record—written, typed, or audio—of how their learning felt and what helped them stay with the work.

Implementation: Reserve three minutes at the end of class. Offer two prompts:

---

44 Aldunate, N., & González-Ibáñez, R. (2017). An integrated review of emoticons in computer-mediated communication. *Frontiers in Psychology, 7*, Article 2061. https://doi.org/10.3389/fpsyg.2016.02061

- What emotion showed up while you worked today?

- What helped you get started or get unstuck?

Every other week, invite students to share one strategy (not a personal story) that they plan to keep using. You can also offer a "strategy menu" for those who feel stuck—breathing, asking for a first step, planning the time, or moving to a quieter space if possible.

Why it Works: Naming feelings, even briefly, can reduce reactivity and help students re-enter thinking with more control.

2. Emotion Check-Ins

Description: Class opens with a short, optional check-in that normalizes feelings and invites focus.

Implementation: Use one prompt most days for consistency: a single word for "how I'm arriving," a 1–5 energy slider, or an emoji. Always pair it with a plan cue: What's your first step today? Accept responses by voice, chat, or private message; no one is required to disclose.

Why it Works: Students see that emotions are welcome and manageable and move directly from naming to action.

3. Role-Playing Scenarios

Description: Students practice language for tense moments—misread chat, one voice dominating, a group member going quiet—while the stakes are low.

Implementation: Create three brief scenarios that mirror your class. In trios, students take roles and practice a simple sequence: ask to clarify → restate what you heard → invite correction → propose a next step. Debrief the whole group: Which phrases helped? What will you borrow next time?

Why it Works: The class gains shared language for repair and disagreement, which keeps collaboration humane and on track.

4. Mindfulness Activities

Description: Short, predictable resets help students regulate attention and return to the task after interruptions at home.

Implementation: Use a 60–90 second routine at transitions: three slow breaths; a brief head-to-hand scan; or a "reset and plan" cue—breathe in, name your next step, begin. Keep it optional and neutral.

Why it Works: Brief, regular practice is associated with small-to-moderate benefits for stress in school settings.

5. Emotional Charades

Description: Students nonverbally act out common classroom emotions so peers can practice recognition and supportive responses.

Implementation: Prepare cards with feelings that show up in learning (confused, impatient, relieved, proud, overwhelmed). In small groups, one student draws a card and silently acts out the corresponding feeling for 15–20 seconds. Peers guess, then name a class situation that could bring on that feeling, and one helpful response.

Why it Works: Students expand their emotion vocabulary and link feelings to concrete classroom moves.

6. Digital Storytelling Projects

Description: Students share short stories of learning, challenge, or change using a medium that fits them—video, audio-over-slides, or illustrated posts.

Implementation: Offer a focused prompt: Tell a two-minute story about a time you learned something the hard way, or describe a moment you changed your mind. Share first in stable peer groups, then curate a class reel. Emphasize choice and boundaries: students decide how much to reveal, and the focus stays on what the experience taught them.

Why it Works: Story builds empathy, voice, and belonging without demanding personal exposure.

7. Group Discussions on Emotions

Description: The class takes up one theme that affects learning—asking for help early, coping with deadlines, or handling disagreement online.

Implementation: Frame the topic in one minute, then use round-robin turns or chat to gather brief contributions. Close with a tangible takeaway: each student writes one strategy they will try this week.

Why it Works: Students see that common challenges are shared, and they leave with a plan they chose.

8. Virtual Support Circles

Description: Voluntary, structured sessions create a safe place to name challenges and receive respectful listening.

Implementation: Meet weekly or biweekly for 15–20 minutes with clear agreements: confidentiality, speaking from "I," passing allowed, and no advice without permission. Students share a current challenge and one step they might take; peers offer a brief reflection or appreciation. Provide referral paths to counselors or supports when needed.

Why it Works: Trust grows when students know there is a regular time and place to be heard.

9. Emotional Awareness Workshops

Description: Short, skills-focused sessions connect basic neuroscience and practical tools students can use immediately.

Implementation: Invite a counselor or trained educator to teach stress physiology, help-seeking, and regulation strategies (breathing, "name it to tame it," planning the first step, sleep, and screen habits). Pair each idea with a brief practice and a simple handout.

Why it Works: Students see emotions and learning as linked and leave with specific, repeatable moves.

10. Reflection and Goal-Setting

Description: Students look back at how emotions and strategies shaped their learning and set a realistic next goal.

Implementation: At the end of a unit or term, prompt three questions:

- Which emotion showed up most for you in this course?

- What helped you keep going when the work was hard?

- What will you try next time to start sooner or ask for help earlier?

Students write one concrete goal and, if appropriate, choose a peer or adult to keep them accountable.

Why it Works: Reflection turns experience into learning; small, specific goals carry it forward.

Conclusion

Emotions are not a detour from learning; they are the road students take to reach it—especially online, where tone is thin, distractions are plenty, and help can be hard to ask for.

When we give emotions a simple place in the routine—through quick check-ins, brief resets, and shared repair language—and teach students to move from what I feel to what I'll do next, we make it easier for them to enter the work and stay with it.

Two practical anchors support that stance. First, make intentions explicit and teach repair; we cannot assume text will carry tone as we expect, a point long demonstrated in email studies of miscommunication. Second, keep guidance about online life balanced and evidence-aware, drawing on current public-health advisories while you help students build real skills for self-management.

Small, steady moves are enough. When we keep them visible and humane, students bring more of themselves to the task—and the task becomes more reachable.

Reflection Questions

- When did you feel most emotionally steady during online work this week, and what made that possible?

- Which routine—check-in, reset, or repair script—helped you participate when things got bumpy?

- What is one change (by you or by us) that would make it easier to ask for help early?

Discussion Prompts (For Staff Meeting)

- Where do misreads most often occur in our courses (chat, comments, email)? What short scripts could we adopt, across classes, for quick repair?

- Which participation options (voice, chat, short post, audio note) are working well for our learners? Where do we need an additional pathway?

- How will we share balanced guidance about social media with families—grounded in current advisories—without panic or stigma?

Chapter 5: Developing Empathy and Social Awareness

Introduction

Empathy and social awareness are not add-ons to learning; they're the way we hold one another up while we do hard things. These skills matter even more in an online classroom—where we meet through messages, cameras, and shared documents. When we understand what someone else might be feeling or what they might be bringing into class that day, we make room for patience, clearer conversation, and genuine collaboration.

In today's interconnected world, students move between cultures, languages, and experiences with every click. They work with peers they may never meet in person, and they read words that arrive without tone or expression. If we want that space to feel safe and fair, we have to teach students how to listen for what isn't said, check their assumptions, and respond with care. That is empathy in practice, and it can be learned.

This chapter stays practical. We'll look at simple techniques you can model to help empathy grow—ways to slow the rush of judgment, invite fuller listening, and name the feelings that shape a conversation. We'll add activities that let students try on perspectives different from their own, so curiosity becomes a habit and not a rare moment.

We'll pay attention to peer interactions, because classmates are powerful teachers: group roles, feedback routines, and discussion structures can turn everyday work into practice for social awareness. And we'll open the classroom to the world beyond it by using digital platforms for community service and issue-based projects. When students see how their voices can help others, empathy evolves from an idea to a responsibility.

Our aim is steady and humane: help students understand one another a little better each week, so the room—on screen or in person—feels kinder, clearer, and more workable. When empathy and social awareness are woven into how we learn, students don't just complete assignments; they build relationships that make deeper learning possible.

Evidence from a large cluster randomized trial of the Roots of Empathy program[45] with 8–9-year-olds found improvements in social–emotional outcomes, underscoring the value of explicit empathy practice in schools (Connolly et al., 2018 – open PDF).

Techniques for Fostering Empathy in Students

1. Modeling Empathy

Students learn how to treat one another by watching how we treat them. When we respond with patience, name emotions without judgment, and keep our promises, we teach more than any slide can carry.

In a digital classroom, this shows up in small, steady ways: acknowledging a late arrival without shaming it, crediting

---

[45] Richards, D., & Viganó, N. (2019). *Digital technology and teacher stress: Impact of school conditions and the role of coping strategies* [Unpublished manuscript]. Queens University Belfast.
https://pureadmin.qub.ac.uk/ws/portalfiles/portal/147926461/3013046.pdf

students' ideas by name in the chat, and circling back to someone whose camera is off to check privately whether they need an alternative way to participate.

Practical Application:

- Start with language that validates without prying: "Thanks for sharing that. I hear that you're frustrated, and that makes sense. Let's take this one step at a time."

- Narrate your own empathic moves briefly so students can copy them: "I'm going to pause and read that question again to make sure I understand it the way you meant it."

- Close tough moments with repair: "I think my reply sounded sharper than I intended. Let me restate more clearly."
  These habits create a tone that students will borrow with one another.

2. Encouraging Active Listening

Active listening is more than staying quiet while someone else talks. It is paying attention to words, pace, and what might be unsaid—and then checking that you understood before you add your view. This skill prevents many small misreads from turning into big ones in online discussions.

Practical Application:

- Teach a three-step mini-sequence students can use anywhere: Listen → Reflect → Respond.

Listen: focus on the speaker or post; no multitasking.

Reflect: offer a one-line summary: "So you're saying the deadline felt tight and made the writing rushed—did I get that right?"

Respond: add a question, agreement, or gentle challenge.

- In chat-based discussions, ask every student to "reflect first" by replying with "What I heard was…" before they argue or agree.

- Rotate a "listening lead" role during group work: one student's job is to capture the speaker's main point and feeling before the team moves on.

3. Empathy Mapping

An empathy map helps students step outside themselves and consider what someone else might think, feel, notice, and need. It works well with literature, case studies, current events, or classroom conflicts you want to unpack safely.

Practical Application:

- Use four simple quadrants on a shared document: Sees / Thinks / Feels / Needs.

- Give a short scenario (real or fictional) and ask groups to fill in each quadrant with concrete, text-based clues rather than guesses about motives.

- End by asking students to write one supportive action that would respect what the person feels and answer what they need.

- Keep maps anonymous when the scenario is sensitive; the goal is understanding, not putting a spotlight on anyone's story.

4. Literature and Storytelling

Stories invite students to feel with someone before deciding what to think about them. That shared emotional ground makes tough conversations kinder and more honest. In digital spaces, stories can be read, heard, or watched—and students can contribute their own in formats that feel safe and secure.

Practical Application:

- Choose short texts or excerpts with clear emotional stakes and varied perspectives. Pair the reading with two questions:

One: "Where did you feel with the character?"

Two: "What choice did they make that you understand even if you don't agree?"

- Offer multiple ways to respond—voice note, brief post, or a 60–90 second video reflection—so students can choose a comfortable entry point.

- Invite "micro-stories" from students: a moment they changed their mind, helped someone, or received help. Keep it optional and set boundaries about what not to share. The focus stays on what the moment taught, not on private details.

5. Role-playing and Perspective-taking

Role-play allows students to rehearse difficult conversations while the stakes are low. It also surfaces language that protects dignity when disagreements arise online.

Practical Application:

- Give pairs a simple script frame to keep things safe and purposeful:

A: describes the situation and feeling in one sentence. **B:** reflects and asks a clarifying question. **C:** proposes a need (*time, clarity, help, space*). **D:** offers one action they can take to meet that need.

- Use familiar school scenarios: a group member not contributing, a message that sounded rude, a classmate talking over others.

- Debrief with two prompts: "Which phrase helped?" and "What would you change next time?" Capture helpful phrases in a shared doc titled "Language We Can Use," and refer back to it during real class work.

Why These Techniques Work Together

Modeling sets the tone; active listening keeps the signal clear; empathy mapping and stories widen students' view; role-play turns insight into language they can use the very next period. Run a few of these consistently—don't try to do them all at once—and you'll feel the room shift: fewer misreads, more patience, and a stronger sense that everyone is trying to understand before they judge.

Activities that Promote Understanding of Diverse Perspectives

1. Cultural Exchange Projects

What it Is: Students share pieces of their lives—traditions, languages, food, music, or family stories—and learn how classmates' experiences shape how they see the world.

Practical Application:

- Host short, rotating "culture spotlights" during the first 10 minutes of class once a week. Invite volunteers to bring a photo, artifact, song clip, or recipe and explain why it matters to them.

- Build a shared digital gallery where each student posts one item and a 3–4 sentence caption. Encourage classmates to comment with questions rather than judgments.

- Offer opt-in formats: written post, audio note, or brief video, so students can choose the medium that feels respectful of home and family.

2. Diversity Discussions

What it is: Guided conversations about topics like race, gender, language, disability, socioeconomic experience, and migration—handled with care and clear norms.

Practical Application:

- Establish three visible agreements: listen to understand, speak from personal experience, and critique ideas without labeling people.

- Use focused prompts that keep the discussion grounded: a short news piece, a poem, or an image. Ask students to name what they notice, what they wonder, and what connects to their own experience.

- Close with a written reflection: "One thing I learned," and "One question I'm still holding." This gives quieter students a voice and helps you gauge the temperature of the room.

3. Documentary and Film Analysis

What it Is: Short documentaries, news features, or narrative clips that put students in contact with lives unlike their own.

Practical Application:

- Select segments (5–12 minutes) with clear human stories rather than statistics alone. Provide a viewing guide with three lenses: context (who, where, when), perspective (whose voice we hear, whose we don't), and impact (how policies or events land on real people).

- After viewing, use small groups to write two questions they'd ask the filmmaker or the people featured. Bring one question per group to the whole class for discussion.

- Invite a "response of care" option—students draft a brief note, resource list, or next-step idea inspired by what they saw.

4. Community Engagement Projects

What it is: Service-learning that meets a real need and helps students understand local experiences—run in person, online, or as a hybrid.

Practical Application:

- Start with a community partner or a clear issue (food access, parks, elder connection, language support). Define a specific contribution students can make in your time frame: creating multilingual info sheets, recording how-to videos, designing a simple awareness website, or hosting a Q&A with community members.

- Pair every action with reflection: What did we notice? Whose voices guided our choices? What will we hand off so the work continues?

- End with a brief public share—a page on the school site, a community night, or a partner's social post—crediting students and the partner by name.

5. Empathy Interviews

What it is: Students interview people with lived experience of a topic, practicing deep listening and ethical storytelling.

Practical Application:

- Teach the difference between curiosity and intrusion. Students draft respectful questions that invite stories (e.g., "Can you tell me about a time when…?") and avoid "gotcha" or overly personal angles.

- Conduct interviews in pairs: one interviewer, one note-taker. Always secure informed permission, clarify how the story will be used, and offer the interviewee a chance to review quotes.

- Students synthesize what they heard into a short profile or audio postcard that centers the interviewee's voice. Require a final paragraph titled "What I learned and how it changed my view."

These activities widen the circle of who and what students know. When we give them safe ways to share, listen, and act, differences stop being walls and start becoming places to learn.

The Role of Peer Interactions in Developing Social Awareness

1. Collaborative Learning

What it is: Working in small groups gives students daily practice with sharing airtime, negotiating roles, and noticing how their choices affect others.

Practical Application:

- Form groups of three or four and assign clear, rotating roles (facilitator, timekeeper, note-capturer, checker).

- Post a visible goal and timeline for each task so process conflicts don't masquerade as personal ones.

- Built in two checkpoints: midway, the facilitator asks, "Does anyone need a different way to contribute?"; at the end, groups name one behavior to keep **and** one to improve next time.

2. Peer Mentoring Programs

What it is: Older or more experienced students support younger peers, building empathy through guidance, encouragement, and shared problem-solving.

Practical Application:

- Match mentors and mentees by interest area or course needs, not just by age.

- Give mentors a simple session guide: greet, ask a warm-up question, check goals, try one strategy together, and set a next step.

- Keep meetings short (15–20 minutes) and consistent (weekly/biweekly). Provide a private channel for quick questions so mentors can ask for help without exposing mentees.

3. Discussion Circles

What it is: A structured way for students to speak, listen, and reflect on experiences, current events, or class dilemmas while protecting dignity.

Practical Application:

- Set three ground rules everyone can remember: listen to understand, speak from "I", pause before you respond.

- Use a common prompt (e.g., "Describe a time you changed your mind" or "Name a moment you needed help but didn't ask") and a visible order of speakers.

- Close with a one-line reflection: "I felt heard when…" *or* "A point I'm taking with me is…" Collect these to gauge the climate and plan the next circle.

4. Online Collaborative Platforms

What it is: Shared documents, boards, or course spaces that let students plan, draft, comment, and give feedback in real time or asynchronously.

Practical Application:

- Create a project hub for each group with task goals, timelines, roles, decision logs, and feedback space.

- Teach two short feedback stems to keep tone constructive: "One strength I notice is…" and "One suggestion is…" Require every comment to include both.

- Invite multiple participation routes—typed comments, voice notes, or brief screen recordings—so students can choose the format that fits them and the task.

5. Conflict Resolution Activities

What it is: Guided practice that helps students recognize friction early and use language that repairs rather than escalates.

Practical Application:

- Share a four-step script students can keep on hand:

One: Name the issue without blame ("I felt rushed when…").

Two: Reflect what you heard ("You needed the draft sooner, right?").

Three: State a need ("I need clearer deadlines / a quieter role / a second look.").

Four: Offer one concrete next step ("Let's set milestones in the doc now.").

- Rehearse with quick role-plays based on typical class tensions (missed contributions, tone in chat, unequal workload).

- After a real conflict, invite a short repair note in the project hub: what happened, what was learned, and what the group will do differently.

Why Peer Work Matters: When students collaborate with structure, mentor with care, speak and listen in circles, build together online, and handle friction with respect, social awareness stops being an abstract goal. It becomes the way the class functions—on screen and in person.

Engaging with Community Service and Social Issues through Digital Platforms

1. Digital Volunteering Opportunities

What it is: Students contribute real help from wherever they learn—tutoring younger learners online, designing flyers for a local nonprofit, translating short documents, or recording "how-to" videos for community partners.

Practical Application:

- **Find a fit.** Ask partners what would truly help this month, not "in general." Keep the scope small and concrete (e.g., "three 2-minute math explainer videos," "a bilingual FAQ for clinic visitors").

- **Set safeguards.** Use school accounts, never personal numbers; share only first names; get written permission from families and partners; keep all communication inside approved platforms.

- **Match strengths.** Offer roles beyond on-camera work—script writing, editing, graphics, captions, quality checks—so every student can contribute.

- **Close the loop.** Schedule a brief handoff meeting where students present work, receive feedback, and ask what to improve next time. A simple thank-you note from the partner goes a long way.

2. Social-Issue Awareness Campaigns

What it is: Students choose an issue they care about—environmental stewardship, food access, mental health, digital safety—and build a focused campaign that informs and invites action.

Practical Application:

- **Keep it local and doable.** Anchor big issues to concrete, such as nearby needs. "Reduce school lunch waste by 20%" is clearer than "solve climate change."

- **Design for clarity.** Teach a three-part message: what's happening, why it matters here, *and* what we can do this month.

- **Use varied formats.** Short infographics, 60–90 second videos, carousel posts, or a simple microsite—students choose the format that best fits the audience.

- **Measure gently.** Track one or two indicators (pledges, QR scans, participation in a drive) and debrief what moved people and what didn't—no shaming, just learning.

- **Model care.** Remind students that real people live inside every issue; require respectful language, source checks, and consent for all images.

3. Interactive Community Projects

What it is: Students research a local challenge with community members, co-create a small solution, and share it publicly—online, in print, or at a virtual forum.

Practical Application:

- **Co-define the question.** Start with listening sessions: What is the problem from your view? What would help in the next 6–8 weeks?

- **Assign clear roles.** Researchers, interviewers, designers, editors, and presenters. Rotate where possible so students try more than one lane.

- **Build with, not for.** Share drafts early with partners. Ask, What should we change to make this more useful?

- **Create something that lasts.** Toolkits, walkthrough videos, translated checklists, neighborhood resource maps, "how to access" guides—choose formats the partner can keep using after the project ends.

- **Credit all contributors.** Publish a short acknowledgment that names students and community collaborators; archive the project in your LMS so future classes can build on it.

4. Guest Speakers and Virtual Panels

What it is: People with lived experience—organizers, caregivers, small-business owners, artists, public servants—share stories and answer students' questions in a moderated, respectful session.

Practical Application:

- **Prepare the room.** Share brief bios, set norms (listen to understand, ask genuine questions, no recording without permission), and collect questions ahead of time.

- **Balance voices.** Invite panelists who represent different angles on the issue; include youth voices when possible.

- **Plan for impact.** After Q&A, give students five quiet minutes to write what surprised them and one action they could take—however small.

- **Follow through.** Send thank-you notes with one takeaway students remembered from each speaker. If speakers are comfortable, invite them to review any student write-ups before posting.

5. Reflection on Community Engagement

What it is: Students look back on what they did, what they learned about others, and what changed in their own thinking.

Practical Application:

- **Use a simple frame.** *Notice → Name → Next.*

Notice: What did you observe about the people affected by this issue?

Name: What emotions came up for you while doing this work?

Next: What will you do differently the next time you collaborate with a community partner?

- **Offer choices.** Written reflection, audio note, short video, or a conversation in small groups.

- **Connect back to class.** Ask students to identify one skill from the project—listening, translation, conflict repair, plain-language writing—that will help in their next group assignment.

- **Protect dignity.** Remind students to center what they learned rather than "saving" narratives; no sharing of personal details from community members without explicit consent.

When service and issue-based work live inside a digital classroom, empathy becomes visible. Students learn to listen before they decide, to ground big ideas in real needs, and to turn care into contribution. The work doesn't have to be large to matter; it has to be honest, respectful, and useful to someone beyond the class.

Conclusion

Developing empathy and social awareness is essential for fostering social and emotional learning in digital classrooms. Educators can empower students to cultivate empathy, understand diverse perspectives, and build meaningful relationships by implementing effective techniques, activities, and community engagement initiatives.

Evidence from broader lines of research points in the same direction: [46]service-learning is associated with gains in civic attitudes, social skills, and academic indicators, [47]structured contact across differences reliably reduces prejudice in part by increasing empathy and reducing anxiety, and [48]cooperative learning approaches are linked to social and academic benefits when roles and interdependence are clear.

---

[46] Celio, C. I., Durlak, J., & Dymnicki, A. (2011). *A meta-analysis of the impact of service-learning on students* [PDF]. *Journal of Experiential Education, 34*(2), 164–181. https://www.tamiu.edu/profcenter/documents/Meta-AnalysisoftheImpactofSLonStudentts_2011.pdf

[47] Pettigrew, T. F., & Tropp, L. R. (2008). How does intergroup contact reduce prejudice? Meta-analytic tests of three mediators. *European Journal of Social Psychology, 38*(6), 922–934. https://doi.org/10.1002/ejsp.504

[48] Kyndt, E., Raes, E., Lismont, B., Timmers, F., Cascallar, E., & Dochy, F. (2013). *A meta-analysis of the effects of face-to-face cooperative learning: Do recent studies falsify or verify earlier findings?* Educational Research Review, 10, 133–149. https://doi.org/10.1016/j.edurev.2013.02.002

As we continue to explore the integration of SEL in digital thinking classrooms, the next chapters will provide additional insights and strategies for promoting emotional growth and well-being. Together, we can create a comprehensive approach to SEL that equips students with the skills they need to thrive both academically and emotionally.

Reflection Questions

- Think of a recent online discussion. When did you feel most understood, and what helped?

- Describe a time you changed your view after hearing a classmate's perspective. What shifted for you?

- Which sentence starter helps you disagree respectfully online (e.g., "Can I share how I'm seeing this?")?

- In your last group task, which role let you contribute best? Which role will you try next, and why?

- After engaging with a community issue, what did you learn about others—and about yourself?

Discussion Prompts

- How will we keep "listen → reflect → respond" visible in our LMS, shared docs, and chat?

- Where do students need more than one way to participate, and how will we build that in without lowering expectations?

- What norms keep diversity conversations both safe and honest in our context?

- Which local partner or issue could we support in the next 6–8 weeks, usefully and respectfully?

- When conflict shows up in chat or group work, which repair phrases will we adopt as a class?

Chapter 6: Coping Strategies for Digital Learners

Introduction

Online learning asks a lot of students. They juggle deadlines that arrive by notification, sit longer at screens than their eyes or backs prefer, and try to learn without the steady cues of a shared room. It's no surprise that stress, anxiety, and emotional fatigue can pile up.

The medium itself can wear on the body and mind: extended screen use is tied to digital eye strain[49]—headaches, dry eyes, blurred vision—and related discomfort that makes concentrating harder. Sleep[50] can take a hit, too; evening light exposure (especially from devices) disrupts melatonin and circadian rhythms, leaving students more irritable and less focused the next day.

Add the constant ping of interruptions, and attention gets choppy—people often work faster to "catch up," but at the cost of higher stress and frustration[51].

---

[49] American Optometric Association. (n.d.). *Computer vision syndrome: Eye- and vision-related problems from digital device use.* Retrieved October 20, 2025, from https://www.aoa.org/healthy-eyes/eye-and-vision-conditions/computer-vision-syndrome

[50] Harvard Health Publishing. (2018, August). Blue light has a dark side. Harvard Health. https://www.health.harvard.edu/staying-healthy/blue-light-has-a-dark-side

[51] Mark, G., Gudith, D., & Klocke, U. (2008). The cost of interrupted work: More speed and stress. *Proceedings of the SIGCHI Conference on Human Factors in Computing Systems*, 107–110. Association for Computing Machinery. https://doi.org/10.1145/1357054.1357072

This chapter explores practical coping strategies you can implement in class, shares brief student testimonials about what has helped, and closes with tips families can use at home to reinforce the same habits.

We'll keep each move light enough to use every day: brief mindfulness to settle the start of a lesson, structured breaks to reduce screen fatigue, clear time-management routines, supportive peer connections, creative outlets, movement, regular emotional check-ins, and small goal-setting cycles that build a sense of control. Families can support the same rhythms at home with simple, shared tech use and downtime plans.

The aim is straightforward: give students tools that help them feel less overwhelmed and more in charge of their day— so even when the work is demanding and the screen time is real, they can recover their focus, protect their well-being, and keep going.

Understanding the Need for Coping Strategies

Coping strategies aren't a luxury in online learning; they're the guardrails that keep students steady when the road gets busy. The stressors are familiar—and they add up.

- **Academic pressure.** Deadlines cluster in the same week, grades update in real time, and every notification can feel urgent. Large reviews[52] link school-related pressure with higher symptoms of anxiety and low

---

[52] Steare, T., Gutiérrez Muñoz, C., Sullivan, A., & Lewis, G. (2023). *The association between academic pressure and adolescent mental health problems: A systematic review. Journal of Affective Disorders, 339*, 302-317. https://doi.org/10.1016/j.jad.2023.07.028

mood in students; the pattern is strongest around high-stakes timelines.

- **Screen fatigue.** Long stretches at a device strain eyes and attention. Eye-care guidance and reviews describe a common cluster—headaches, dryness, blurred vision, neck/shoulder tension—and recommend short, regular visual breaks (like the 20-20-20 rule) to reduce discomfort.

- **Social isolation.** Some students feel alone even in a full video grid without hallway talk or quick smiles across a table. Public-health and psychology summaries[53] tie weak social connections to poorer mental health; schools are explicitly named as places where connection matters for well-being and performance.

- **Digital distractions.** Multiple tabs, message pings, and split attention make it harder to do deep work. Studies[54] of everyday tech use and multitasking show more interruptions, more stress, and shakier performance when attention is constantly toggled.

---

[53] U.S. Department of Health and Human Services. (2023, May 3). Our epidemic of loneliness and isolation: The U.S. Surgeon General's Advisory on the healing effects of social connection and community [PDF]. https://www.hhs.gov/sites/default/files/surgeon-general-social-connection-advisory.pdf

[54] Mark, G. (2008). *Millennial: Camera-Ready Submission* [PDF]. University of California, Irvine. https://ics.uci.edu/~gmark/Home_page/Publications_files/Millennial%20Camera-Ready%20Submission4.pdf

When we name these pressures clearly, we can teach small, repeatable ways to handle them—brief resets for the body, simple planning routines for time, kinder norms for peer support, and flexible paths back to focus after interruptions. The next sections translate those ideas into moves you can use right away.

Coping Strategies for Digital Learners

1. Mindful Practices

Mindfulness is simply paying steady attention to the moment you're in—breath, body, and thought—without judgment. In class, short, predictable practices help students settle before they start.

Implementation: Open with 60–90 seconds of guided breathing or a brief body scan. Keep the language plain: "Breathe in… breathe out… notice your shoulders." Rotate options (box breathing, five-count exhale, eyes-open soft focus) so it never feels performative. Offer opt-in—students can participate with cameras off or just listen.

Student Voice: "I used to jump into class already stressed. Two minutes of breathing slows me down enough to listen." —Mia, 11th Grade

Why it Helps: School-based mindfulness programs[55] show small-to-moderate benefits for stress and emotion regulation when practices are brief and regular.

---

[55] Zenner, C., Herrnleben-Kurz, S., & Walach, H. (2014). *Mindfulness-based interventions in schools—A systematic review and meta-analysis*. Frontiers in Psychology, 5, 603. https://doi.org/10.3389/fpsyg.2014.00603

2. Structured Breaks

The brain and eyes need pauses. Short breaks prevent strain and help students return with more patience and focus.

Implementation: Every 30-45 minutes, cue a 2–3 minute reset away from the screen: stand, stretch, look out a window. Teach the 20-20-20 habit: every ~20 minutes, focus on something ~20 feet away for ~20 seconds.

Student Voice: "When we take real breaks, I can actually focus again. I stretch, grab water, and I'm ready." —Jason, 10th Grade

Why it Helps: Eye-care guidance recommends brief, regular visual breaks to reduce digital eyestrain.

3. Time Management Techniques

Planning lowers stress. When work is broken into steps, students see progress instead of a wall.

Implementation: Teach a simple weekly plan: list tasks, estimate time, pick the "first bite," and set a 20–25 minute focus timer. Share light templates (today/this week/next) and model how you plan aloud. End work blocks with a one-line log: "What I finished / What I'll start next."

Student Voice: "A planner makes it manageable. I can see what to do first, and it stops the panic." —Sophia, 12th Grade

Why it Helps: Time-planning and monitoring are core self-regulated learning skills[56] linked with better academic outcomes.

---

[56] Zimmerman, B. J. (2002). *Becoming a self-regulated learner: An overview.* Theory Into Practice, 41(2), 64-70. https://doi.org/10.1207/s15430421tip4102_2

4. Supportive Peer Interactions

Feeling backed by classmates reduces stress and keeps students engaged.

Implementation: Use pairs or trios for problem-solving, with quick, rotating roles (facilitator, checker, scribe). Give two feedback stems to keep tone safe: "One strength I notice…" and "One suggestion…". Keep a private Q&A channel so students can ask peers for help without spotlight.

Student Voice: "Working with friends lowers the pressure. We share ideas, and it doesn't feel like I'm stuck alone." — Ethan, 9th Grade

Why it Helps: Youth mentoring and peer-support models[57] show small but meaningful benefits across social, behavioral, and academic outcomes when relationships are consistent and guided.

5. Creative Expression

Art, music, writing, and design give feelings somewhere healthy to go—and give students a win they can see.

Implementation: Offer opt-in creative submissions (poem, sketch, audio snippet, short video) alongside standard responses. Build five-minute "creative pauses" into longer blocks: draw a symbol for your current mood, score a scene with sound, write a two-line micro-story about today's challenge.

---

[57] Raposa, E. B., Rhodes, J. E., Stams, G. J. M., Card, N., Burton, S., Schwartz, S. E. O., Sykes, L. A. Y., Kanchewa, S., Kupersmidt, J., & Hussain, S. (2019). *The effects of youth mentoring programs: A meta-analysis of outcome studies.* Journal of Youth and Adolescence, 48(3), 423–443. https://doi.org/10.1007/s10964-019-00982-8

Student Voice: "When I'm drawing, the noise in my head gets quieter. I come back calmer." —Lily, 11th Grade

Why it Helps: Creative work gives emotions a safe outlet and turns vague stress into something concrete you can make, shape, and finish. That sense of agency (I can create, revise, and complete) lowers tension and restores focus for the next task.

6. Physical Activity and Movement

Movement is a reset button for mood and attention.

Implementation: Add micro-movement between segments: three stretches, ten chair squats, or a one-minute walk. Post optional daily movement prompts that students can do off-camera. Invite short "movement reports" at the end of the week: what they tried, how it felt.

Student Voice: "A quick workout on break lifts my mood. I'm more awake for the hard parts." —Aiden, 10th Grade

Why it Helps: Regular activity[58] is associated with better attention and memory in school-age children and reduced symptoms of low mood.

7. Emotional Check-Ins

Naming a feeling lowers its temperature and makes it easier to choose the next step.

---

[58] U.S. Department of Health and Human Services, Centers for Disease Control and Prevention. (2024, April 3). *Health benefits of physical activity for children.* Retrieved from https://www.cdc.gov/physical-activity-basics/health-benefits/children.html

Implementation: Start class with a low-stakes check-in: a one-word mood in chat or a quick slider poll. Normalize short shares ("anxious," "distracted," "ready") and pair with a plan: "What's one thing that would help you focus for the next 20 minutes?"

Student Voice: "When the teacher asks how we're doing, I feel seen—and I try harder." —Chloe, 12th grade

Why it Helps: Putting a name to what you're feeling reduces the "static" around it and makes it easier to choose a useful next step (ask for help, take a quick reset, start with an easy win). Regular check-ins also show students they're seen, which boosts willingness to engage.

8. Goal Setting and Reflection

Small, clear goals build a sense of control and momentum.

Implementation: Have students set one academic and one personal process goal each week ("submit drafts a day early," "use a 25-minute timer twice"). Revisit on Fridays with three prompts: What moved? What stalled? What's the first step next week? Celebrate process, not just product.

Student Voice: "Writing goals and checking them weekly keeps me steady. Even bad weeks have a next step." —Noah, 11th Grade

Why it Helps: Goal setting and self-evaluation are foundational self-regulation practices tied to improved motivation and achievement.

Light reminders for students (pin in your LMS): drink water nearby, blink often, look far every so often, move a little between blocks, and ask for help earlier than you think you should. These small habits make online days gentler—and make tough tasks feel more possible.

Tips for Parents on Reinforcing Coping Strategies at Home

You don't have to overhaul your whole routine to help your child feel steadier with online school. Small, consistent moves at home make the school day gentler and give them tools they can use on their own.

1. Make a Simple Family Plan for Tech

Agree on a few basics you can stick to: where devices live at night, what "homework mode" looks like, and how you'll handle interruptions during study blocks. Writing it down helps everyone remember—and lowers arguments in the moment. The American Academy of Pediatrics offers an easy Family Media Plan[59] you can tailor to your household.

2. Protect Sleep

Even a good plan unravels if kids are exhausted. Create a "screens down" buffer before bed (aim for 30–60 minutes), dim lights in the evening, and keep phones out of bedrooms

---

[59] American Academy of Pediatrics. (n.d.). How to make a family media use plan. HealthyChildren.org. https://www.healthychildren.org/English/family-life/Media/Pages/How-to-Make-a-Family-Media-Use-Plan.aspx

when possible. Nighttime blue light[60] can delay melatonin and disrupt sleep; small changes here pay off the next day in mood and focus.

3. Build Movement into the Day

Short, frequent bursts of activity lift energy and reset attention. Encourage a quick walk after school, a stretch break between assignments, or a family "move minute" before dinner. Global guidelines[61] recommend about 60 minutes of moderate-to-vigorous activity daily for children and adolescents; that hour can be spread across play, sports, chores, or active transport.

4. Use Light Structure for Time and Tasks

A little planning lowers pressure. Sit with your child on Sunday night to list the week's bigger tasks, then help them choose the "first bite" for each day. During work blocks, encourage a simple timer (20–25 minutes on, short break) and a one-line log at the end: "What I finished / What I'll start next." The goal isn't perfection; it's rhythm.

5. Normalize Short Mindfulness Resets

If your child gets tense before logging on, try a 60–90 second breathing exercise together. Keep it casual—eyes open, slow exhale, a shoulder roll. When you model the reset yourself

---

[60] Sleep Foundation. (2025). How blue light affects kids' sleep. https://www.sleepfoundation.org/children-and-sleep/how-blue-light-affects-kids-sleep
[61] World Health Organization. (2020). WHO guidelines on physical activity and sedentary behaviour. World Health Organization. https://www.ncbi.nlm.nih.gov/books/NBK566046/

("I'm going to take two calm breaths before I answer this email"), you make it feel safe for them to try.

6. Keep Peer Connection Alive

Help them schedule short, purposeful study calls or small group chats so school doesn't feel solitary. For social time, agree on where and when it happens, and teach them to pause if a conversation turns unkind or overwhelming. If you're concerned about online behavior, review cyberbullying prevention guidance[62] and decide together how you'll handle reporting and blocking.

7. Create Gentle Routines around Breaks and Food

Set water within reach. Encourage a real break between classes—stand up, look out a window, grab a snack with protein and fiber. These little rituals signal "reset" to the brain and make it easier to start again.

8. Check In on Feelings without Forcing Big Talks

Once a day, ask something small and specific: "What was one hard moment? What helped even a little?" If they're not ready to talk, offer options: thumbs up/sideways/down, a one-word text, or a shared note you peek at together later. You're building the habit of naming emotions and choosing a next step.

---

[62] U.S. Department of Health and Human Services, StopBullying.gov. (n.d.). How to prevent cyberbullying: A guide for parents, caregivers, and youth [PDF]. https://www.stopbullying.gov/sites/default/files/documents/Cyberbullying%20 Guide%20Final%20508.pdf

9. Learn the Platforms They Use

A quick tour of your child's learning apps (and favorite social platforms) helps you spot friction points—missed notifications, confusing workflows, or chats that need boundaries. Knowing the basics makes your guidance feel relevant and respectful.

10. Know When to Bring in Backup

If worry, low mood, or school avoidance stick around for more than a couple of weeks—or if you see big changes in sleep, appetite, or energy—loop in the school counselor or a health professional. You're not alone, and early support makes a difference.

Conclusion

Equipping digital learners with effective coping strategies is essential for supporting their emotional well-being in an increasingly complex educational landscape. By implementing mindfulness practices, encouraging peer interactions, and fostering a supportive environment, educators and parents can successfully empower students to manage their emotions and navigate challenges.

Brief micro-breaks[63] can also lift well-being and help students sustain effort, and small metacognitive routines—

---

[63] Albulescu, P., Macsinga, I., Rusu, A., Sulea, C., Bodnaru, A., & Tulbure, B. T. (2022). *"Give me a break!" A systematic review and meta-analysis on the efficacy of micro-breaks for increasing well-being and performance.* PLoS ONE, 17(8), e0272460. https://doi.org/10.1371/journal.pone.0272460

planning, monitoring, and adjusting—strengthen confidence and performance.

As we explore social and emotional learning in digital classrooms, the following chapters will provide additional insights and practical strategies for promoting emotional growth and well-being. Together, we can create a comprehensive approach to SEL that equips students with the skills they need to thrive both academically and emotionally.

Reflection Questions

- Which single routine from this chapter would help you most this week, and why?

- What tends to knock you off course—timing, task size, or emotion? Which small move could catch you earlier?

- Name one feeling you notice before you lose focus. What's a 60-second reset you'll try when it shows up?

- Which peer role helped you contribute best this month? Which role will you try next?

- What's one way you can make your study space kinder to your body and eyes?

Discussion Prompts

- How will we make breaks real (away from screens) and re-entry smooth?

- Where can we offer two participation paths without lowering expectations?

- What will our class language be for repair when tone or chat goes sideways?

- Which "first bite" planning routine will we all use so students see consistency across classes?

- How will we involve families in two or three small habits that matter most?

Chapter 7: Encouraging Growth Mindset and Resilience

Introduction

In the ebb and flow of digital learning, glitches happen, plans shift, and even confident students can feel thrown off. In that space, two ideas steady the room: you can grow and recover.

A growth mindset helps students see skill as something they build, not something fixed. Resilience gives them a way back when a tab freezes, an assignment misses the mark, or feedback stings: pause, adjust, try again.

This matters online because many of the small cues that soften struggle in a physical classroom—the quick check-in, the shared smile—are easier to miss on a screen. Without those cushions, a rough first attempt can feel final.

When we make effort visible, normalize re-tries, and model calm resets, students learn to carry themselves through the bumps instead of waiting to be rescued. You see the shift in ordinary moments: a student posts a question sooner, another resubmits without shame, a group owns a misstep and revises the plan.

A warm, steady approach is also credible. Large-scale work[64] with high-schoolers has shown that brief, well-designed online

---

[64] Yeager, D. S., Hanselman, P., Walton, G. M., Murray, J. S., Crosnoe, R., Muller, C., Tipton, E., Schneider, B., Hulleman, C. S., Hinojosa, C. P., Paunesku, D., Romero, C., Flint, K., Roberts, A., Trott, J., Iachan, R., Buontempo, J., Yang, S. M., Carvalho, C. M., Hahn, P. R., Gopalan, M., Mhatre, P., Ferguson, R.,

mindset activities can lift grades and nudge students toward more advanced coursework—evidence that the message *effort grows ability* can travel through a screen when it's concrete and well-timed. And the resilience field reminds us that adaptation is not rare heroism; it's "ordinary magic[65]"—everyday protective habits and relationships that we can actually build in school routines.

We'll keep this chapter close to practice. We'll explore the importance of a growth mindset in digital classrooms, share strategies for nurturing resilience without turning class into therapy, and demonstrate how to celebrate both the efforts and the successes so that effort feels worthwhile. The goal isn't to add more to your list; it's to make the list steadier—clear language, humane expectations, and small, repeatable moves that help students keep going.

The Importance of a Growth Mindset in Digital Learning Environments

A growth mindset is the quiet belief that *I can get better at this*—and that the path to "better" runs through effort, strategies, and support. In online spaces, where a frozen screen or a baffling interface can feel like a verdict on your ability, that belief keeps students moving. Below, we stay with your five threads and show how each plays out on a screen—and in the small choices you and your students make every day.

Duckworth, A. L., & Dweck, C. S. (2019). A national experiment reveals where a growth mindset improves achievement. *Nature, 573*(7774), 364–369. https://doi.org/10.1038/s41586-019-1466-y

[65] Masten, A. S. (2001). *Ordinary magic: Resilience processes in development* [PDF]. https://ocfcpacourts.us/wp-content/uploads/2020/06/Ordinary_Magic_Resilience_Process_000935.pdf

1. Embracing challenges

When students meet a new platform, a tougher rubric, or code that won't compile, a growth mindset reframes the moment: this is practice, not proof. You can bake that stance into the class by narrating your own learning ("I haven't used this feature before—watch how I test it"), by chunking first steps ("let's just upload one file together"), and by crediting the *attempt* as part of the grade. In digital rooms, that gentle nudge toward curiosity is the difference between closing the tab and trying again.

2. Perseverance in the face of setbacks

Glitches and distractions are part of online learning. Students with a growth mindset see setbacks as information, not identity. You can make perseverance practical with simple re-try structures: quick feedback, a specific next step, and a short window for revision. When a student hears, "You're close; run the check again and resubmit by tomorrow," they learn that progress is expected—and possible. Over time, those small recoveries add up to resilience.

3. A positive attitude toward learning

In virtual spaces, mood travels through text and tone. Growth-mindset language helps you keep the atmosphere constructive without sounding soft: "First drafts do the heavy lifting," "Skills grow with use," "Let's find the part that can move today." Pair that language with visible progress markers—checklists, mini-milestones, "first bite" tasks—so students can see effort turning into momentum. As they watch themselves advance, the work feels less like judgment and more like discovery.

4. Increased motivation

Believing that effort changes outcomes fuels the willingness to start, to stick, and to return after an interruption. You can spark that motivation with tiny, frequent wins: a 10-minute focus sprint that earns a green check, a "most improved process," shout-out; a rubric line for *strategy use* (planning, asking for help early, revising after feedback). Motivation, especially online, grows where students can *see* their own growth.

5. Collaboration and peer support

Digital courses run on collaboration—shared docs, threaded comments, quick huddles. A growth mindset turns group work from "who's good at this?" into "how do we help each other get better?" Keep roles light and rotating; normalize coaching language ("What move helped you?" "Try my first step."); and log decisions where everyone can see the learning curve. As students swap strategies instead of labels, the class culture shifts from comparison to collective progress.

Why does this matter?

Decades of work on mindsets[66] link the belief that abilities can grow with greater persistence and willingness to take on

------

[66] Dweck, C. S. (2016). Mindset: The new psychology of success (Updated ed.). Random House Publishing Group.
https://www.penguinrandomhouse.com/books/44330/mindset-by-carol-s-dweck-phd/

challenge, especially when feedback is process-focused rather than person-focused.

Large, national studies[67] suggest that students holding stronger growth beliefs tend to achieve more—even in the face of economic disadvantage—pointing to the protective role these beliefs can play across contexts. And recent syntheses[68] emphasize that mindset messages work best when they're concrete (specific strategies), timely (right when a challenge appears), and embedded in everyday instruction—the exact conditions you can create in a digital class.

Strategies for Nurturing Resilience Among Students

Resilience grows in ordinary moments. In digital classrooms, it sounds like a student taking one steady breath before a quiz loads, asking for the "first step" instead of going silent, or returning to a draft after feedback stings. The strategies below keep your original sequence and stay practical, with warm teacher language and classroom-ready routines— no theatrics, just small habits students can repeat.

1. Teaching self-compassion

Students often speak to themselves in ways they would never use with a friend. When a platform glitches or a first attempt falls flat, the inner script can turn harsh: I'm terrible at

---

[67] Claro, S., Paunesku, D., & Dweck, C. S. (2016). *Growth mindset tempers the effects of poverty on academic achievement.* Proceedings of the National Academy of Sciences of the United States of America, 113(31), 8664–8668. https://doi.org/10.1073/pnas.1608207113

[68] Yeager, D. S., & Dweck, C. S. (2020). *What can be learned from growth mindset controversies?* American Psychologist, 75 (9), 1269–1284. https://doi.org/10.1037/amp0000794

this… I'll never get it. You can show another way. Name what's happening. This is hard, and hard is allowed — and model a kind next step: I'm going to take one slow breath, then reopen the rubric, and try the first paragraph again. Invite students to borrow that script in chat or in their notes.

Over time, they learn to notice, normalize, and choose—three moves that make returning to the work possible. Research on self-compassion links this kinder stance to healthier coping and greater persistence in learning; it's not indulgence, it's fuel for trying again.

2. Setting realistic goals

Online tasks can feel endless when they arrive as a stack of tabs. Shrinking the field into "first bites" lowers the urge to avoid. Work with students to turn "do better" into something doable: By Wednesday, finish the outline; on Friday, add two pieces of evidence.

Keep the plan visible in your LMS and revisit it briefly at the end of class: What moved today? What starts first next time? Classic goal-setting research[69] is clear: specific, challenging goals paired with feedback and strategies increase effort and persistence. In practice, that looks like a crediting process (planning, asking early, revising) alongside the product, so effort has somewhere to land.

---

[69] Locke, E. A., & Latham, G. P. (2002). Building a practically useful theory of goal setting and task motivation: A 35-year odyssey. *American Psychologist, 57*(9), 705-717. https://doi.org/10.1037/0003-066X.57.9.705

3. Encouraging growth-mindset language

Students take their cues from how we talk about struggle. Keep your feedback anchored in process and strategy: Your evidence is solid; next, tighten the claim by naming the pattern you saw. Avoid labels, good or bad.

When a student says, "I'm just not a math person," reflect back with a path: "You're early in this skill; let's try a different first step." In digital spaces, this precision matters because tone gets flattened. Concrete, strategy-focused responses are easier to read as support rather than judgment, and point the way back to action.

4. Modeling resilience

Let students see you recover. If your screen freezes, narrate a calm reset: I'm refreshing the page; while that loads, I'm writing our next step in chat so we don't lose the thread. If an activity lands awkwardly, own it and adjust: That didn't quite work. Here's what we'll change and why.

Short, matter-of-fact modeling lowers the emotional cost of trying for everyone. Students learn that a misstep isn't a verdict; it's information. The message is simple: we act, we learn, we revise.

5. Fostering a supportive community

Resilience is easier in a company. Build light structures that make it normal to ask for help and to offer it. Rotate roles during group work so everyone has a way in—facilitator, timekeeper, summarizer, checker—and keep a shared notes doc where decisions and next steps live. Credit ideas by name so contributions are visible.

When students practice these routines across tasks, peer support becomes part of the air of the class. Decades of cooperative learning research[70] tie these structures to better relationships and stronger engagement—both protective factors when work gets tough.

6. Promoting problem-solving skills

Panic narrows options; a simple sequence widens them. Teach[71] a short loop students can use whenever they're stuck: state the snag → list two options → pick one → test for five minutes → if still stuck, ask with a screenshot and what you tried. A "show your tries" note is required when they request help, so coaching has traction.

After assessments, hold a brief "mistake clinic": each student chooses two errors, names the pattern, and practices one new strategy for each. This kind of explicit strategy instruction is a reliable route to stronger, more transferable learning.

---

[70] Roseth, C. J., Johnson, D. W., & Johnson, R. T. (2008). *Promoting early adolescents' achievement and peer relationships: The effects of cooperative, competitive, and individualistic goal structures.* Psychological Bulletin, 134(2), 223–246. https://doi.org/10.1037/0033-2909.134.2.223

[71] Dunlosky, J., Rawson, K. A., Marsh, E. J., Nathan, M. J., & Willingham, D. T. (2013). *Improving students' learning with effective learning techniques: Promising directions from cognitive and educational psychology.* Psychological Science in the Public Interest, 14(1), 4-58. https://doi.org/10.1177/1529100612453266

Pulling the pieces together

Across these strategies, the rhythm is the same: notice the moment, choose a kinder script, shrink the task, lean on the group, and try one concrete move. Nothing here requires extra software or long detours. What it does require is consistency—steady language, visible planning, familiar roles, and a problem-solving loop students can run on their own.

Over weeks, you hear the change. Students ask for the "first bite" instead of saying they're lost. They point to a strategy they tried before asking for a fix. They speak to themselves with a little more grace. That's resilience you can feel; it travels well—on-screen or in the room.

Celebrating Failures and Successes in the Learning Process

Failures and wins both teach. Online, where a rough first try can feel permanent, we make learning safer by showing students how to learn from mistakes and noticing their subsequent progress. The five moves below keep your original framing and add just enough structure to work smoothly in a digital class.

1. Reframing failure as a learning opportunity

When a draft misses the mark, treat the result as information, not identity. Point to one thing that worked, one thing to change, and the next concrete step. Short, directional feedback ("where you're going, how you're doing, what to do next") helps students re-enter the work instead of shutting down.

- **Class move:** After returning work, give two minutes for students to write a single "fix it" action, then act on it immediately (revise one paragraph, redo one problem).

- **Why it helps:** Task-focused feedback[72] outperforms vague praise or criticism and strengthens achievement.

2. Creating a celebration of learning

Make improvements visible so the effort feels worth it. Celebration here is practical: we spotlight what changed, not who ranked highest.

- **Class move:** At the end of a unit, host a short "Show & Tell the Change" gallery: each student posts before/after snapshots (one slide, two screenshots) with a caption naming the specific improvement.

- **Why it helps:** Calling attention to concrete gains builds momentum and keeps students oriented toward progress rather than perfection.

3. Encouraging reflection on growth

Reflection turns a step forward into something students can repeat. Keep it brief and specific.

- **Class move:** Use a two-question exit prompt after major tasks: What changed in your work this time? What will you try first next time? Collect responses in

---

[72] Hattie, J., & Timperley, H. (2007). *The power of feedback.* Review of Educational Research, 77(1), 81-112. https://doi.org/10.3102/003465430298487

your LMS so students can see their own patterns over weeks.

- **Why it helps:** Guided, focused reflection (naming what changed and the next step) strengthens metacognition[73] and improves transfer and attainment.

4. Sharing stories of resilience

Real examples make perseverance feel normal. A short story—yours, a peer's, or a figure from history—shows that detours happen and that strategy, not talent labels, moves us forward.

- **Class move:** Keep a rotating "Resilience Corner" in your course space. Each week, one student posts a 3–4 sentence note: the stumble, the strategy used, and the small win.

- **Why it helps:** Narratives lower the stigma around mistakes and give classmates language for their own recoveries.

5. Implementing growth-mindset challenges

Design low-stakes challenges that reward trying, revising, and persisting. The point is to practice "not yet"—and to see effort change results.

---

[73] Quigley, A., Muijs, D., & Stringer, E. (2018, April 27). *Metacognition and self-regulated learning: Guidance report.* Education Endowment Foundation. https://educationendowmentfoundation.org.uk/education-evidence/guidance-reports/metacognition

- **Class move:** Run a two-week "one skill, many tries" challenge. Students choose a specific micro-skill (e.g., tighter claims, cleaner citations, debugging steps), log three attempts, and submit a final snapshot showing what improved. Recognize the process—early help-seeking, strategy use, and revision—alongside the product.

- **Why it helps:** Well-timed mindset activities[74], including brief online modules, can increase persistence and outcomes when they are concrete and embedded in classwork.

Kept simple, these routines send a steady message: errors are raw material, effort moves skill, and progress—however small—deserves notice. Over time, students start to speak that language back to you and to one another, and the class becomes a place where trying again is just what we do.

Conclusion

Encouraging a growth mindset and resilience among students is essential for their success in digital learning environments. When we make effort visible, normalize retries, and teach calm recovery, students begin to see challenges as part of learning rather than a verdict on their ability.

By implementing effective strategies—modeling resilience in real time, guiding students to set clear goals, teaching a

---

74 Paunesku, D., Walton, G. M., Romero, C., Smith, E. N., Yeager, D. S., & Dweck, C. S. (2015). *Mind-set interventions are a scalable treatment for academic underachievement.* Psychological Science, 26(6), 784–793. https://doi.org/10.1177/0956797615571017

simple problem-solving loop, and celebrating both the missteps and the improvements—we help them approach difficult work with steadier confidence.

As you weave these practices into daily routines, you'll notice small but important shifts: Students ask for the "first step" instead of going silent, they try again more quickly after feedback, and they lean on one another with more ease. Those moments add up. They strengthen attention, persistence, and collaboration—the very capacities online learning demands.

As we continue to explore the integration of social and emotional learning in digital classrooms, the following chapters will provide additional insights and practical strategies for promoting emotional growth and well-being. Together, we can create a supportive environment where students thrive academically and emotionally, equipped with the skills to navigate the complexities of their educational experiences.

Reflection Questions

- When did you most *feel* a growth mindset in your class this week? What language or routine sparked it?

- Think of a recent stumble (tech glitch, missed rubric line, confusing step). What did you try first? What will you try next time?

- Which feedback phrase do you use most—does it name process/strategy clearly enough for students to act?

- Where do students most often get stuck online (starting, persisting, revising, asking for help)? What one routine could lower that friction?

- How are you making small gains visible (before/after snapshots, progress logs, "most improved process" notes)? What's one way to show progress more consistently?

Discussion Prompts

- Share a brief story of a re-try that changed the outcome (assignment, quiz, presentation). What made the turnaround possible?

- Compare two feedback moves you've used (e.g., "good job"/"needs work" vs. "one thing working, one thing to change, next step"). What did students do differently afterward?

- Draft a 10-minute "mistake clinic" you can run after the next assessment. What will students analyze, and what will they practice immediately?

- Identify one place in your LMS to surface progress (checklist, mini-milestones, before/after slides). What will students update, and how often?

- Role-play a 60-second modeling moment: your screen freezes or an activity flops. Narrate a calm reset. What wording keeps the room steady and teaches recovery?

Chapter 8: Engaging Families in SEL

Introduction

School doesn't end when the screen turns off. The way a child is listened to at dinner, the words a caregiver chooses after a rough day, and the quiet routines that hold a household together. All this shapes how a child shows up to learn.

In digital classrooms, where the line between home and school is thinner, families aren't just "in the loop"; they are part of the learning environment itself. When we invite parents and guardians in as true partners, students feel steadier. They carry skills from class into daily life and bring family strengths back into the room.

Family partnership is not about perfect schedules or elaborate programs. It grows from small, consistent habits: a teacher who explains *why* a new routine matters, a parent who asks a gentle follow-up question instead of rushing to fix, a shared phrase that helps everyone pause before reacting.

These moments teach emotional skills as clearly as any lesson plan. Children watch how adults handle stress, repair after a misunderstanding, and show kindness when time is tight. They copy what we model.

Digital tools make this easier when we use them with care. A short message in plain language can do more than a long newsletter. A five-minute video recorded on a phone can show families what "emotional check-ins" look like better than a page of instructions.

A simple two-question poll can tell us when families need a different meeting time or a translated resource. The goal is not to ask families to do school at home but to share a few practices that fit naturally into family life—ideas that work at the breakfast table, on the walk to the market, or during a quiet moment before bed.

We also keep equity at the center. Not every home has the same time, bandwidth, or devices. Some caregivers work nights. Some students live across two households. Many families speak languages beyond the school's primary language.

When we offer flexible ways to connect—text, email, short videos, PDFs, and office hours at varied times—we make partnership possible for more people. When we invite families to tell us what already works for their child, we honor expertise that has been there all along.

Partnership goes both ways. Families need clear and kind information about what their children are learning socially and emotionally—what words we use in class, how we handle conflict, and how we encourage students to steady themselves when things are hard.

Educators, in turn, need to hear what children are practicing at home, what stresses are present, and which routines calm or spark them. When that exchange is regular and respectful, students get a coherent message: The adults in my life are on the same team.

As the educational landscape evolves, the role of families in supporting students' social and emotional learning (SEL) becomes increasingly vital. Parents and guardians are essential partners in fostering emotional intelligence, resilience, and interpersonal skills in their children.

Engaging families in SEL initiatives not only enhances students' emotional well-being but also strengthens the home-school connection. This chapter examines the crucial role of parents and guardians in fostering SEL at home, outlines tools for communicating and collaborating with families digitally, and explores strategies for establishing a community of support around SEL initiatives.

The Role of Parents and Guardians in Supporting SEL at Home

Families shape the emotional "weather" children bring to class. The way a parent listens after a hard day, the words a guardian chooses during conflict, and the small routines that hold a home together all teach skills we practice in school—naming feelings, steadying ourselves, and caring for others.

Below are six ways families can nurture SEL at home, with simple, everyday examples.

1. Modeling emotional intelligence

Children learn first by watching us. When adults show how they notice a feeling, choose a steadying move, and repair after a misstep, kids see that emotions are workable—not something to hide.

Try this: narrate quietly in the moment: "I'm getting frustrated with this form. I'm going to breathe and try again," then come back and say what helped. Over time, that script becomes a child's inner voice.

Why it matters*: Responsive, back-and-forth adult–child interactions—the "serve and return[75]" of daily life—build the foundation for self-regulation and social skills that support later learning.

2. Encouraging open communication

A child who can say "I felt left out" or "I'm overwhelmed" is already halfway to problem-solving.

Try this: make a five-minute check-in part of the evening rhythm. Ask open questions ("What feeling showed up today?" "What helped a little?"). Validate first, fix later.

Why it matters: When adults coach[76] emotions—naming, accepting, and guiding—children show stronger self-regulation in early grades.

3. Reinforcing school SEL skills in daily routines

Home is where classroom language becomes habit.

Try this: during chores or games, spotlight empathy and teamwork: "You noticed your sister was stuck and offered a

---

[75] Center on the Developing Child at Harvard University. (n.d.). *Serve and return: Back-and-forth exchanges.* https://developingchild.harvard.edu/key-concept/serve-and-return/

[76] Wilson, B. J., Petaja, H., Yun, J., King, K., Berg, J., Kremmel, L., & Cook, D. (2014). *Parental emotion coaching: Associations with self-regulation in aggressive/rejected and low-aggressive/popular children. Child & Family Behavior Therapy, 36*(2), 81–106. https://doi.org/10.1080/07317107.2014.910731

turn—that's kindness and problem-solving." Use the same brief prompts students hear at school ("Name the feeling; name one next step").

Why it matters: Core components[77] of effective SEL—identifying one's own and others' feelings, social skills, and coping strategies—are most powerful when practiced across settings.

4. Setting clear, kind expectations for behavior

Consistency lowers stress. Children thrive when they know how your family communicates and repairs.

Try this: co-write a short family agreement (6–8 plain-language lines) about respect, devices, and how you'll handle conflict ("We pause before posting; we apologize and make a plan"). Revisit one line each week.

Why it matters: Partnership[78] approaches that align home and school expectations are linked to better social, emotional, behavioral, and academic outcomes.

5. Encouraging resilience without over-rescuing

Protecting kids from every stumble can unintentionally shrink their confidence. Standing nearby while they try again grows it.

---

[77] Lawson, G. M., McKenzie, M. E., Becker, K. D., Selby, L., & Hoover, S. A. (2019). *The core components of evidence-based social and emotional learning (SEL) programs.* Prevention Science, 20(4), 457–467. https://doi.org/10.1007/s11121-018-0953-y

[78] Sheridan, S. M., Kim, E. M., Coutts, M. J., Sjuts, T. M., Holmes, S. R., Ransom, K. A., & Garbacz, S. A. (2012). *Clarifying parent involvement and family-school partnership intervention research: A preliminary synthesis (CYFS Working Paper No. 2012-4)* [PDF]. Nebraska Center for Research on Children, Youth, Families & Schools (CYFS), University of Nebraska–Lincoln. https://www.cyfs.unl.edu/resources/downloads/working-papers/CYFS_Working_Paper_2012_4.pdf

Try this: after a setback—a tough grade, a missed goal—ask, "What did you learn?" and "What's your first step now?" Offer help as a menu ("feedback from the teacher, a study buddy, or a new plan?"), and then praise the effort and the strategy they chose.

Why it matters: Parent engagement[79] that focuses on coaching and reflection (rather than doing the task for the child) supports readiness and social–emotional growth, especially for students facing disadvantage.

6. Fostering belonging at home

Belonging is the everyday sense of "these are my people." It grows in small, predictable moments.

Try this: Protect a simple ritual—shared breakfast on weekdays, a weekly walk, or story time where everyone brings one "high" and one "low." Keep it short and consistent so it sticks even on busy weeks.

Why it matters: Family involvement[80] and warm connections are associated with higher engagement and healthier social–emotional development across ages.

---

[79] Sheridan, S. M., Knoche, L. L., Edwards, C. P., Bovaird, B., & Kupzyk, K. A. (2010). *Parent engagement and school readiness: Effects of the Getting Ready intervention on preschool children's social-emotional competencies. Early Education and Development, 21*(1), 125-156. https://www.ncbi.nlm.nih.gov/pmc/articles/PMC3967127/

[80] Martínez-Yarza, N., Solabarrieta-Eizaguirre, J., & Santibáñez-Gruber, R. (2024). The impact of family involvement on students' social-emotional development: The mediational role of school engagement. *European Journal of Psychology of Education, 39*(4), 4297-4327. https://doi.org/10.1007/s10212-024-00862-1

Quick note for schools: Families[81] want to know *what* SEL looks like and *how* to help. Brief, plain updates (common phrases used in class, a two-line home prompt, a 60-second demo video) respect time and make partnership doable. Surveys suggest educators sometimes underestimate how interested caregivers are in the SEL work happening at school—ask, don't assume.

This is the heart of home partnership: We keep language simple, make routines doable, and trust that small, repeated moments teach big skills. When families and schools send the same message—feelings are workable, effort changes outcomes, repair is part of relationships—students carry that steadiness with them, on-screen and off.

Tools for Communicating and Collaborating with Families Digitally

In today's digital age, steady, two-way communication between home and school is essential for students' social and emotional growth. The goal isn't more messages; it's clearer, kinder ones that help families feel informed, invited, and able to act. The tools below make that partnership doable, even on busy weeks.

1. Communication platforms (one home base, not five)

Pick a primary channel—your LMS inbox, Remind, ClassDojo, Seesaw, or another district-approved tool—and

---

[81] Drew, A. L., Hill, A., & Whitmire, K. (2024). What do parents know about social-emotional learning in their children's schools? Gaps and opportunities for strengthening intervention impact. Heliyon, 10, Article e2400391. https://www.sciencedirect.com/science/article/pii/S2773233924000391

stick with it so families aren't hunting across apps. Keep messages short, specific, and focused on what a caregiver can do next ("We're practicing naming feelings; try asking, 'What feeling showed up today?' at dinner").

When possible, enable translation and SMS so families without reliable internet still receive updates.

Make it easy: a weekly "three-line note" (what we're practicing, one sentence on why it matters, one question to ask at home) builds trust without flooding phones.

Why this works: Brief, consistent teacher-to-parent messages[82] have been shown to boost student engagement and reduce course failure, especially when they name a concrete action caregivers can take.

Design tip: Evidence syntheses on parental engagement[83] stress clarity, feasibility, and alignment with learning—keep asks small and practical.

2. Virtual parent-teacher conferences (flexible and focused)

Video meetings remove travel barriers and can bring more caregivers into the conversation. Offer a few time windows (including one early morning or early evening slot), share a two-minute agenda in advance, and begin with a genuine

---

[82] Kraft, M. A., & Rogers, T. (2015). *The underutilized potential of teacher-to-parent communication: Evidence from a field experiment.* Economics of Education Review, 47, 49–63. https://doi.org/10.1016/j.econedurev.2015.04.001

[83] Education Endowment Foundation. (2018). *Working with parents to support children's learning: Guidance report.* Education Endowment Foundation. https://d2tic4wvo1iusb.cloudfront.net/production/eef-guidance-reports/supporting-parents/EEF_Parental_Engagement_Guidance_Report.pdf

strength before discussing needs. Close with one agreed next step for school and one for home.

Make it easy: Send a simple "conference prep" card outlining what your child is learning, one question you might ask, and how we'll measure progress together.

Helpful guidance: The U.S. Department of Education's Parent and Family Digital Learning Guide[84] outlines practical ways to prepare families for virtual conversations and co-problem-solve around learning goals and safety.

3. Interactive class website or family portal (a calm, single source of truth)

A light, living page can answer most "What's happening?" questions: weekly learning focus, key dates, class norms, short "how to help at home" prompts, and links to translation or accessibility supports. Keep the layout clean; prioritize plain language and mobile-friendly viewing so families can check it on a phone between shifts.

Make it easy: update on the same day each week; archive past updates so caregivers can catch up quickly.

Why this matters: Family–school frameworks emphasize building capacity on both sides. They give families clear, usable information and invite their expertise back into the classroom.

---

[84] **U.S. Department of Education. (2020).** *Parent and family digital learning guide.* Office of Educational Technology.
https://www.education.nh.gov/sites/g/files/ehbemt326/files/inline-documents/sonh/parent-and-family-digital-learning-guide.pdf

4. Online workshops and webinars (light, practical, and recorded)

Short virtual sessions—15–30 minutes—are often all families can spare. Focus on one skill (emotion coaching, helping with planning, creating calm homework routines), model it once, and share a one-page takeaway. Record the session and post the link so caregivers who work evenings don't miss out.

Make it easy: co-host with your counselor or a community partner; invite questions in advance so the session meets real needs.

Helpful guidance: Federal family-engagement resources offer plain-language tips for supporting digital learning at home. Link them on your class site so caregivers can revisit on their own time.

5. Thoughtful social media use (connection without compromise)

If your school uses social channels to celebrate learning, protect privacy, and keep the focus on community—not on students' identities or personal details. Obtain consent (or offer clear opt-outs), avoid sharing last names or schedules, and never post when a student opts out. When in doubt, share student work products without faces or post general class updates instead.

Make it easy: pin a "community posting" policy at the top of your class page and model how to celebrate effort ("We saw brave revising today!") rather than ranking students.

Safety first: Neutral, classroom-friendly checklists can help educators and families think through privacy[85], consent, and boundaries before posting.

Keep the tone human. Whether it's a quick text, a five-minute video chat, or a one-page resource, families are far more likely to engage when communication is consistent, respectful of time, and tied to something they can actually do tonight.

Building that kind of partnership is less about the app and more about the stance: a clear purpose, small and doable steps, and a genuine invitation to participate in the learning.

Creating a Community of Support Around SEL Initiatives

When families, schools, and community partners row in the same direction, students feel it. Expectations line up. Language feels familiar across home and the classroom. Support doesn't stop at the bell.

Building that kind of community isn't about grand programs; it's about inviting more adults to share the work of helping young people feel safe, seen, and capable—and giving them simple ways to join in.

---

[85] Common Sense Education. (n.d.). *Keeping your students (and yourself) safe on social media: A checklist.*
https://www.commonsense.org/education/articles/keeping-your-students-and-yourself-safe-on-social-media-a-checklist

1. Partner with local organizations (make support visible and close to home)

Community groups—youth centers, libraries, faith-based organizations, mental health providers, cultural associations—already serve the children you teach. A short list of trusted partners, shared with families in clear language, can turn "Where do we go for help?" into "Here's who we can call."

Start with one focus (for example, stress management or mentoring), co-host a brief virtual session, and follow with a one-page resource in multiple languages. Over time, those touchpoints build a web of care around students.

Why this helps*:* Strong SEL implementation is most durable when practices are coordinated across classrooms, homes, and community settings, and when families[86] are treated as authentic partners rather than recipients.

2. Form an SEL family-school team (shared planning, shared language)

Invite a small, diverse group of caregivers, teachers, counselors, and—when age-appropriate—students to meet regularly. Keep meetings practical: review a simple dashboard (attendance patterns, climate pulse, translation needs), co-create two short family resources for the next month (for example, a "how we repair after conflict" script and a "naming feelings" prompt), and decide how to gather feedback.

---

[86] Collaborative for Academic, Social, and Emotional Learning (CASEL). (n.d.). *Family partnerships.* CASEL. https://schoolguide.casel.org/focus-area-3/family-partnerships/

Rotating meeting times, child care during in-person sessions, and virtual options widen the circle.

Why this helps: Family–school partnership standards[87] emphasize shared decision-making and two-way communication as core to student success; teams make those principles concrete.

3. Host community-facing SEL events (small, welcoming, and repeatable)

Rather than a single big night, offer short, themed gatherings across the year—"Calm Homework Routines," "Supporting Friendship Skills," "First Steps After a Tough Grade." Pair a 15-minute demo with a brief practice and a take-home card. Invite a community partner to co-facilitate, and provide translation and recordings to enable more families to participate.

Why this helps: A steady focus on relationships and connectedness[88]—built through frequent, two-way communication and approachable learning opportunities—supports well-being and sustained engagement.

4. Lift student leadership (let young people help carry the message)

Create a student SEL council or fold SEL into an existing leadership group. Students can help script short "how we do it

---

87 National PTA. (n.d.). *Family-school partnerships.* https://www.pta.org/home/run-your-pta/family-school-partnerships

88 Centers for Disease Control and Prevention. (2024, December 3). *Enhance connectedness among students, staff, and families.* https://www.cdc.gov/mental-health-action-guide/strategies/enhance-connectedness.html

here" videos (for example, how your class runs check-ins or repairs misreads online), welcome families at events, and mentor younger peers in routines like respectful discussion or planning the "first step" after feedback. When students teach the skills, ownership grows on every side.

Why this helps: Developmental relationships[89]—adults expressing care, challenging growth, sharing power, and expanding possibilities—are proven engines for youth thriving; student leadership activates all four.

5. Keep a simple feedback loop (listen, adjust, tell people what changed)

Families engage more when they can see their voice matter. Use one short survey each term (five items, mobile-friendly) and a two-question pulse after events ("What was useful?" "What should we change?"). Post a "You said / We did" note on your class site: "You asked for earlier office hours; we added a 7:45 a.m. slot." That visible responsiveness builds trust.

Why this helps: Decades of family-engagement work underline the payoff of clear, feasible asks and responsive communication; aligning information to family needs increases participation and impact.

---

[89] Search Institute. (2018). *Developmental Relationships Framework.*
https://www.search-institute.org/wp-content/uploads/2018/05/Developmental-Relationships-Framework_English.pdf

6. Connect support to everyday places (library desks, clinic counters, faith halls)

Not every caregiver can attend a school event. Share one-page SEL guides (plain language, translated, with QR codes to short videos) through libraries, pediatric clinics, food pantries, and community centers. Ask partners to keep a small stack on hand. Meeting families where they already are respects time and widens access.

Why this helps: Collaborating with the community[90] to expand learning opportunities and services is a core standard for effective family–school partnerships.

Building a community around SEL is less about adding work and more about aligning it: common words for feelings, simple ways to repair, shared expectations for how we treat one another. When families, schools, and community partners move together, students get the same steady message everywhere they turn—that consistency is what helps them grow.

Conclusion

Engaging families in social and emotional learning is crucial for fostering a stable, supportive environment where students can thrive. When parents and guardians model empathy, keep communication open, and practice small daily routines that mirror classroom language, children carry those skills between home and school.

---

[90] National PTA. (n.d.). *Standard 6—Collaborating with community: Assessment guide*. https://www.pta.org/docs/default-source/files/programs/national-standards-for-family-school-partnerships/assessment_guide_standard_6.pdf

When educators use clear, accessible digital tools and invite feedback that genuinely shapes the next steps, families feel like partners, not bystanders. And when schools connect this work to community resources, the web of support around each child gets stronger and more visible.

By recognizing the vital role of parents and guardians, utilizing simple and reliable channels for collaboration, and expanding a broader community of support, we make SEL more consistent and humane. The result shows up in everyday moments: a child who names a feeling instead of shutting down, a family who knows how to help after a hard day, a class that repairs quickly and gets back to learning.

As we continue to explore SEL in digital thinking classrooms, the next chapter turns to assessment—how we can understand students' growth in practical, respectful ways, and how data can guide instruction without reducing children to numbers.

Taken together, this family–school partnership and a thoughtful approach to measurement create a coherent path forward: one community, speaking a shared language, helping every student thrive academically and emotionally.

Reflection Questions

- Which family communication habit (text update, short video, three-line note) do you feel most able to sustain every week, and why?

- Where might translation, timing, or device access be getting in the way for some caregivers—and what's one adjustment you can make this month?

- Think of a recent home–school exchange. What language choices helped a caregiver feel respected and capable? What would you revise next time?

- Which classroom SEL routine (check-ins, repair language, goal-setting) could benefit from a simple home prompt? Draft the single sentence you'll share.

- Whose voices are missing from your current family feedback loop? Name one step to invite those caregivers (e.g., a different channel, time, or partner).

- When families shared a strategy that works at home, how did you bring it back into class? What's one way to credit and reuse that insight this week?

Discussion Prompts

- Share a brief example of a "small, repeatable" home practice (a nightly check-in, a shared ritual) that strengthened a student's steadiness in class. What made it doable?

- Compare two communication approaches you've tried (e.g., weekly SMS vs. monthly newsletter). What did caregivers engage with, and what will you keep or change?

- In triads, draft a family agreement line you could suggest to caregivers (plain language, one sentence) about devices, respectful talk, or repair after conflict.

- Map your community partners (library, clinic, youth center, faith group). Where could a one-page SEL guide or short recorded demo be posted so families can actually see it?

- Role-play a virtual conference opening: one genuine strength, one need, and one shared next step for home and school. What wording felt most human and clear?

- Design a You said / We did note that you could post next week. What feedback will you honor publicly, and what small change will you make visible?

Chapter 9: Assessing SEL in Digital Classrooms

Introduction

As social and emotional learning (SEL) becomes part of everyday teaching, we also need clear, humane ways to understand how students grow. In digital classrooms, checklists and grades rarely tell the whole story.

We see progress in quieter places: a student who asks for help sooner, a group that repairs a misread in chat and keeps working, a class that returns to focus after a glitch. In this context, assessment isn't about labeling students; it's about noticing what's getting stronger, spotting where support will help, and adjusting how we teach so every learner feels seen.

Because online spaces can blur cues, we benefit from tools that make social and emotional growth visible without overwhelming teachers or students. Thoughtful SEL assessment blends three kinds of evidence:

- what students say about their own skills and experiences (brief self-reflections and surveys);

- what we can observe in routines and collaboration (clear, behavior-based rubrics);

- and what our digital platforms can summarize over time (lightweight trend data on participation and follow-through).

When those pieces come together, the picture is useful and respectful. Educators get timely signals to guide instruction, students get language for their progress, and families can understand how to support at home.

Several practical resources can help you choose and use assessments that fit your context. The SEL Assessment Guide[91] (developed with RAND and the SEL Assessment Work Group) explains what common tools measure and how to put results to work in schools—especially when combining student self-reports with observations and climate data.

CASEL's assessment[92] pages compile vetted instruments and selection tips so you can match tools to age, purpose, and setting rather than starting from scratch. And large, real-world efforts—such as the California CORE Districts' student-report surveys[93]—show that short, well-designed self-reports can produce reliable, actionable information about skills like growth mindset, self-management, and social awareness when they're implemented thoughtfully.

In the sections that follow, we'll keep the focus practical: ready-to-use tools and rubrics you can adapt for your class, routines that build student self-reflection into the week, and

---

[91] Taylor, J. J., & Hamilton, L. S. (2019, March 28). *How do you measure social and emotional learning?* RAND Corporation.
https://www.rand.org/pubs/commentary/2019/03/how-do-you-measure-social-and-emotional-learning.html
[92] Collaborative for Academic, Social, and Emotional Learning (CASEL). (n.d.). *Assessment tools.* https://casel.org/state-resource-center/assessment-tools
[93] Gehlbach, H., & Hough, H. J. (2018, May). *Measuring social emotional learning through student surveys in the CORE districts: A pragmatic approach to validity and reliability* [Report]. Policy Analysis for California Education.
https://edpolicyinca.org/publications/measuring-social-emotional-learning-through-student-surveys-core-districts

brief case examples of schools using SEL assessment to strengthen both teaching and climate in digital settings.

Examples of Assessment Tools and Rubrics for Measuring SEL

In digital classrooms, we still look for the same things we value in person: growing self-awareness, steadier self-management, kinder collaboration, and choices that reflect care for self and others.

What changes online is how we see the growth. The tools below make SEL visible without turning class into a survey factory. They're practical to run, light on prep, and designed to feed instruction rather than label students.

1. Self-assessment Surveys

What it looks like: Short check-ins (5–8 items) students complete in your LMS or a secure form. Prompts tap the five SEL areas (e.g., "I asked for help when I needed it," "I stayed calm enough to try again after a tech glitch").

How to use: Run a baseline in week one, then a brief pulse every few weeks. Share only class-level patterns with students ("Most of us felt rushed in group work; next time we'll set clearer roles").

Why it helps: When students judge their own strategies against clear ideas of quality, motivation, and achievement can rise[94], especially if they revise work in response.

---

[94] Andrade, H., & Valtcheva, A. (2009). Promoting learning and achievement through self-assessment. *Theory Into Practice, 48*(1), 12–19. https://doi.org/10.1080/00405840802577544

2. Behavioral Rubrics

What it looks like: A simple rubric attached to collaborative tasks, written in student-friendly language (e.g., *Listening:* "Waits, summarizes, and builds"; *Contribution:* "Offers one idea and one question"; *Repair:* "Names a misread and resets respectfully").

How to use: Introduce the rubric briefly, then use it in two ways: self-check at midpoint and teacher snapshot at the end. Keep ratings low-stakes; focus on one glow/one grow.

Why it helps: Clear criteria plus timely feedback are a powerful[95] mix for learning; formative use of rubrics aligns with evidence that feedback clarifies the gap between 'where I am' and 'where I'm going'.

3. Peer-assessment Tools

What it looks like: Two or three prompts students use to respond to a partner or team (e.g., "One moment I felt heard was…," "One suggestion for clearer roles is…"). Run it through your LMS discussion or a quick form; keep names visible so gratitude can be returned.

How to use: Model one exchange live, then give pairs three minutes to post and two minutes to plan one change they'll try next.

---

[95] Hattie, J., & Timperley, H. (2007). The power of feedback. *Review of Educational Research, 77*(1), 81–112. https://doi.org/10.3102/003465430298487

Why it helps: Well-designed peer feedback builds self-regulation: students compare work to criteria, decide next steps, and monitor progress.

4. Journals and Reflection Portfolios

What it looks like: Short weekly reflections (150–200 words or a 60–90-second audio note) attached to a task: "What helped you persist?" "Where did communication break down, and how did you repair it?" Every few weeks, students tag entries to the five SEL areas.

How to use: Offer two prompt choices each week; accept text or audio; respond with one sentence and one question. At midterm, students select three entries and write a brief "learning letter" to themselves.

Why it helps: Reflection strengthens self-regulation[96]—planning, monitoring, and adapting strategies—which is teachable and tied to achievement.

5. Digital Assessment Platforms

What it looks like: Light-touch check-ins embedded in tools you already use (e.g., a two-item poll at lesson end; a rubric column in a shared doc for *collaboration*). Some platforms let you visualize class patterns over time so you can adjust routines.

How to use: Decide on one SEL focus per month (e.g., *asking for help early*). Build one micro-item into a recurring

---

96 Zimmerman, B. J. (2002). Becoming a self-regulated learner: An overview. *Theory Into Practice, 41*(2), 64–70. https://doi.org/10.1207/s15430421tip4102_2

activity (exit ticket, quiz reflection). Report back on what you changed because of what students said.

Why it helps: Treating assessment [97]as for learning—frequent, low-stakes, immediately useful—it has a long record of improving outcomes, especially when it informs next steps rather than simply scores.

Quick build tips (to keep it humane and doable)

- Keep every SEL measure brief and tied to an action you will take in response.

- Share only class-level trends with students unless a learner invites one-to-one feedback.

- Rotate focus: one competency per month is plenty.

- Let students see their own progress over time (a small line chart in your LMS portfolio or a simple "then/now" reflection).

The Importance of Student Self-reflection in the Assessment Process

In a digital classroom, so much of the real work happens off camera—between a paused video and a new draft, in the moment a student decides to try again, in the quiet choice to

---

[97] Black, P., & Wiliam, D. (1998). Inside the black box: Raising standards through classroom assessment. *Phi Delta Kappan, 80*(2), 139–148.
https://www.michigan.gov/-
/media/Project/Websites/mde/2017/09/18/Inside_The_Black_Box_-
_Black_and_William.pdf?rev=da79305095b64f1881d473deac26acd2

ask for help. Self-reflection is how students make that invisible learning visible to themselves.

A few honest lines—what helped, what got in the way, and what they'll try next—turn a finished task into a step forward. Reflection also gives you clearer signals for tomorrow's instruction without adding more screens or longer assignments. The aim isn't long journals; it's brief, regular check-ins that connect feelings, choices, and evidence of learning.

1. Promoting Self-awareness

Self-awareness begins with noticing patterns: When does focus slip? Which cues bring it back? How do emotions shape effort? In digital spaces, students can capture those patterns quickly:

"I drifted during the second video; switching to captions and jotting a three-word summary per minute brought me back."

When students write one sentence like this at the end of a task, they begin to recognize triggers (noise, multitasking, unclear goals) and identify countermeasures (captions, outlining, asking for a model). Over weeks, those small observations become a personal playbook. That is the first move in self-regulated learning: setting an internal cue for *notice* → *adjust* rather than waiting for a grade to tell them something went wrong.

Practical ways to seed self-awareness online: add a single reflection box to the submission page ("What helped you stay with it today?"); open a live class with one emotion word plus one plan (*"anxious → outline first"*); or pin a short "How I learn best" statement in the LMS for students to revise monthly. Keep the prompts steady so noticing becomes routine.

2. Encouraging Personal Growth

Grades arrive after the moment. Reflection keeps growth visible *during* the work. When a student compares a draft to clear criteria—then writes one next step in plain language— effort turns into change they can see: "Criteria say 'use two sources and explain the link to your claim.' I added the second source; next, I'll connect it to the claim with one sentence that begins 'This shows…'"

That small, criteria-referenced move is powerful because it ties improvement to something the student controls. Research on student self-assessment[98] shows that when learners check their work against explicit success criteria and plan a revision, the next draft improves, and motivation rises—students can connect actions to outcomes.

To make this doable in a digital course, attach two prompts to any graded task: "Name one thing you changed to meet the criteria," and "Name your first next step." Accept text or a 30– 60-second audio note. Respond with one sentence and one question; let the revision show the rest.

---

[98] Andrade, H. L. (2019). A critical review of research on student self-assessment. *Frontiers in Education, 4*, 87. https://doi.org/10.3389/feduc.2019.00087

Over time, students build a record of micro-gains—clearer topic sentences, tighter evidence, calmer re-entry after a tech glitch—that grades alone never capture.

3. Fostering Accountability

Online participation can feel fuzzy. Self-reflection, tied to shared norms, makes it concrete. Instead of "I participated," students cite evidence: "I replied to my group within our 24-hour window," "I credited sources with working links," "I asked one clarifying question before submitting."

Those specifics shift the story from impression to behavior. They also make fairness visible in group work: a student who quietly carries the project can point to written evidence of role fulfillment without calling anyone out, and a quieter student can show steady contributions even if they speak less on camera.

This is the goal-monitor–adjust loop at the heart of self-regulation: learners set a target, track actions against it, and choose a next step. The routine is teachable and benefits all students, not just the naturally organized ones; a brief summary of that framework is useful when explaining *why* you're asking for reflection.

A light structure helps: agree on two or three class norms you can actually observe online (timely replies, evidence with links, repair after misreads). Add a single self-check line to the weekly work, where students point to one action that met a norm and one they will improve next time. Keep it low-stakes; the aim is ownership, not policing.

4. Enhancing Communication Skills

Reflection teaches students to turn experiences into clear, neutral language—what happened, how it affected others, what will change next time. That clarity reduces friction in text threads and makes peer support more useful.

Compare the vague "Group work was hard" to the actionable "We skipped roles, so two of us drafted the same part; next time I'll ask to assign a summarizer and checker." The second version invites help and prevents repeat mistakes.

These are the core moves in formative assessment: learners generate feedback for themselves, compare to criteria, and articulate next steps. When students practice that loop regularly, teacher feedback goes further because it lands on a plan the student already owns.

Nicol and Macfarlane-Dick[99] outline seven principles that support this kind of self-regulation; two you can implement immediately are (a) clarifying good performance with concrete criteria and (b) creating opportunities for students to close the gap between current and desired performance.

Make space for voice and accessibility here: offer reflection by text or audio; allow a choice of "write it out" or "record it in 60 seconds." For multilingual students, sentence starters help: "One thing that went well was... Because of that, next time I will..." Tone matters, too—model neutral,

---

[99] Nicol, D. J., & Macfarlane-Dick, D. (2006). Formative assessment and self-regulated learning: A model and seven principles of good feedback practice. *Studies in Higher Education, 31*(2), 199–218. https://doi.org/10.1080/03075070600572090

nonjudgmental language so students learn to separate the person from the behavior.

5. Creating a Culture of Continuous Improvement

A reflective culture is built in small, predictable steps. Keep the cadence light and steady: two lines at the end of class, one sentence attached to a submission, a weekly "what I'll try first" note. The message becomes unmistakable: progress is normal here.

Students see that what they write changes what you do—maybe you shorten the next video, provide a sentence frame, or build in a 90-second reset because many reported screen fatigue.

That feedback loop—clear goals, visible criteria, quick reflection, named next step—functions as the engine of improvement in many contexts.

A few rituals help the culture take root without taking more time:

- **Revision intention.** Before resubmitting, students post one change they made and why it matters.

- **Friday look-back.** One sentence on a skill that moved (e.g., "I asked for help earlier this week and finished faster").

- **Class adjustment note**: Please post a brief "What I'm changing next week because of your reflections" so students feel heard and continue writing honestly.

As the weeks stack up, the benefits show in quieter ways: fewer last-minute panics, more specific questions during office hours, kinder repair after misreads in chat, and a steadier willingness to try again after a bump. Reflection doesn't lengthen the course; it smooths the path through it.

Practical Exercises for Self-reflection

A steady routine of short, well-scaffolded reflections helps students turn feelings and observations into next steps. In digital classes, these moments don't need to be long to be powerful; they need to be clear, predictable, and tied to the work at hand. Below are four exercises from your draft, expanded so you can drop them straight into your course flow.

1. Emotion Check-in

An emotion check-in is a short, predictable moment in which students name how they are arriving and what they need to get started. In a digital classroom, you can place a simple prompt at the top of your LMS agenda or in the chat at the start or close of a session. Invite students to choose a word that fits their current state—calm, wired, unsure, overwhelmed—and add one line about what would help them focus.

Offer a private option (direct message or a short form) so students can participate without posting publicly. The value of this routine lies not in dramatic sharing but in clarity: students learn to recognize their state and pair it with a small plan, while you gain a quick read to adjust pacing, grouping, or instructions.

What makes the check-in work is consistency and a visible response. A sentence from you—"A lot of us are feeling pulled in too many directions; let's break the task into a first ten-minute step and check back"—signals that feelings are data, not a detour.

Over time, students begin to anticipate that move for themselves. The practice stays brief, kind, and predictable; it lowers the emotional "cost of entry" to the lesson and helps the class settle into the work without forcing disclosure.

2. Weekly Reflection Journals

Weekly journals turn scattered impressions into a trackable story of growth. Set up a recurring, low-stakes submission in the LMS with two steady prompts and one that changes with the unit. The steady prompts can stay simple: "One move that helped me persist this week was… because…" and "One moment I'd handle differently next time is… and here's how I'll try it."

The unit prompt invites specificity tied to current work—how students chose evidence, handled disagreement in discussion, or managed distractions during a longer task. Offer flexible formats: a short paragraph, a 60–90 second audio note, or a brief video. The point is to make reflection accessible, not burdensome.

Close the loop by responding with a single sentence and one question, and letting journals influence your next steps. If many students name the same sticking point—confusion about criteria, screen fatigue near the end of a session, uneven group roles—say what you will change and then do it.

Midway through the term, ask students to tag two journal entries that show a shift in their process and write a brief synthesis of what changed. This turns the journal into evidence they can point to, rather than a private diary no one reads.

3. Goal-setting Reflections

Goal-setting reflections help students move from intention to action. At the start of a project or week, ask each student to write one process goal and one product goal. A process goal might be, "I will draft in fifteen-minute intervals and pause to compare my work to the criteria after each interval."

A product goal might be, "My analysis will include two counter-examples and a sentence that explains how they sharpen my claim." Mid-week, invite a short check-in: what moved, what stalled, and one adjustment for the next work block. At the end of the cycle, students submit a "goal audit" alongside their final piece—a short note that names which strategies they kept, which they dropped, and what they would carry forward.

This routine keeps attention on choices students control: how they plan, how they check their progress, and how they respond when something doesn't work. It also gives you concrete material for feedback. Instead of general comments on "effort," you can speak directly to the strategies a student tried and suggest the next small tweak.

In group projects, invite teams to set one shared process goal and one shared product goal, then write a two-or three-sentence debrief on how well those goals guided the work. That small structure layer prevents repeating the same bottlenecks in the next collaboration.

4. Group Reflection Discussions

After a team task—whether a shared document, a design sprint, or a discussion—build in a short debrief that focuses on process rather than personalities. In breakout rooms, each group opens a shared note and responds to three prompts: something the team did that moved the work forward, a friction point that slowed them down, and one concrete change they will try next time.

Rotate the note-taker so that responsibility is spread across the team, and set a clear time box to keep the conversation practical. When the class reconvenes, ask for two or three takeaways across groups and name one class-level adjustment you will make before the next team assignment.

This reflection helps students separate people from patterns. Instead of "group work was hard," they can say, "We didn't assign roles, so two of us drafted the same section; next time we'll choose a summarizer and a checker before we start."

In a digital setting, that kind of specificity prevents misunderstandings in chat threads and reduces the rework that follows. Saving these debrief notes in the LMS creates a living record: students can glance back before the next task and avoid the same missteps, and you can see where a quick mini-lesson or template would make the next round smoother.

Case Studies Showcasing Successful SEL Assessment Strategies

1. An Urban Middle School's SEL Implementation

In a diverse, high-enrollment middle school, teachers agreed on a short list of SEL outcomes they wanted to see more often in day-to-day work: students naming needs, collaborating fairly, and repairing misreads online. They built a simple assessment loop around those goals.

Every Monday, students completed a two-minute self-check on self-management and belonging; during group work, teachers used a common rubric for collaboration (listening, turn-taking, role clarity); on Fridays, students wrote a brief "what changed this week" reflection and selected one piece of work that showed progress.

Because everyone used the same tools, patterns emerged quickly. Teachers noticed that many groups stalled on unassigned roles, so they introduced a one-page roles template and adjusted the collaboration rubric to include "decision recorded and visible."

Over a term, staff reported fewer conflicts during group tasks, and students' reflections shifted from general feelings ("I was stressed") to specific strategies ("I asked for the instructions again, and that helped me restart"). The school didn't try to score emotions; they tracked behaviors tied to learning and used the data to tweak routines. Families received a monthly one-page update describing the classwide adjustment and how to support it at home.

2. A Rural High School's Digital SEL Initiative

A small high school serving a wide geographic area moved much of its instruction online during the winter weather months. Teachers wanted to know whether students felt connected enough to ask for help, and whether group projects were fair when partners lived miles apart.

They added three light pieces to their LMS: (a) a weekly pulse check ("I felt heard this week: 1–5"), (b) a short peer feedback form after team tasks ("one thing your partner did that moved the work forward"), and (c) a reflection tag students attached to any resubmission ("what I changed, and why").

The information was formative, not punitive. Staff used it to implement practical changes, including wider reply windows for discussion posts, flexible ways to contribute (via voice or text), and a rotating "checker" role to balance the workload.

Students reported that group work felt fairer and that it was easier to ask for clarification without embarrassment. Attendance in optional help sessions grew once teachers began each session with the most common pulse-check concern from that week and a concrete fix.

3. SEL in a Fully Remote District Setting

When a district pivoted to fully remote instruction, a cross-grade team created an "assessment map" so SEL wouldn't be swallowed by logistics. They chose three collection points that fit naturally into existing work: a one-question exit ticket after live classes ("What helped you stay with the task today?"). A collaboration rubric was used across subjects, and a quarterly student self-inventory was aligned with five competencies.

School counselors and teachers reviewed the patterns together every three weeks and posted a brief "what we're changing next" note to students.

Two insights stood out. First, many students struggled to re-enter after a tech glitch. Teachers responded by scripting 60-second resets at predictable times and naming the first step back into the task. Second, students' sense of belonging dipped in classes with long stretches of teacher talk.

Staff adjusted pacing—shorter segments, quick "you try" moments, and named turn-taking in chat. Over time, self-inventories showed more students reporting confidence in asking for help, and teachers described fewer "silent" meetings. The district kept the map light and focused; the goal was always to inform instruction, not to rate students.

4. Incorporating Family Feedback in SEL Assessment

An elementary school sought a fuller picture of students' social–emotional growth by inviting families into the assessment loop. Twice each term, families received a two-minute survey with four prompts: "My child felt connected to a classmate/teacher this month," "One strategy that helped at home," "One place my child needs support," and "One question for us."

Teachers paired the family view with students' self-reflections and class rubrics, then shared a classwide adjustment and a simple at-home practice (for example, a two-step plan sentence stem families could try during homework).

This approach improved alignment between home and school. Families felt seen and were more likely to share what worked in their context (quiet start rituals, visual checklists, movement breaks).

Teachers, in turn, used that knowledge to shape small in-class routines that respected different needs. The school was careful with language and privacy, framing the surveys as a way to fine-tune support rather than evaluate children. Participation climbed because the feedback clearly led to visible change.

Adapting these models to your class: Across settings, what worked was modest and repeatable: choose a few behaviors tied to learning, gather light information where students already work, review it on a rhythm, and make one visible change at a time.

Conclusion

Assessing social and emotional learning in digital classrooms isn't about scoring feelings. It's about noticing patterns, listening to students' own accounts of their growth, and making small, visible adjustments that help everyone learn with more steadiness and care.

When we pair light-touch tools (such as self-checks, clear rubrics, and short reflections) with regular opportunities to act on what we learn, students begin to see assessment as support rather than judgment. They can name what's working, ask for what they need, and take the next step with confidence.

The practices in this chapter—self-assessment surveys, behavior rubrics, peer feedback, journals and portfolios, and simple digital check-ins—give you a practical way to keep SEL present without overwhelming your syllabus.

Most of all, they help you and your students focus on the process: The daily moves that build self-awareness, strengthen relationships, and make ethical choices feel doable in online spaces.

As we continue to explore the integration of SEL in digital thinking classrooms, the next chapter will provide insights into engaging families in the SEL process and fostering collaboration between educators and families. Together, we can create a supportive environment that empowers students to thrive emotionally and academically.

Reflection Questions

- When you look at your current assessments, where could a short self-reflection help students connect effort to outcome more clearly?

- Which behaviors (listening, turn-taking, asking for help, repairing misreads) matter most for learning in your class, and how will you make them observable in a rubric?

- What's one small way you can "close the loop" each week—sharing what you heard from students and the single change you'll try next?

- How will you protect dignity and privacy while still gathering the information you need?

Discussion Prompts

- Share a moment when a student's self-reflection changed how you taught the next lesson. What did you adjust, and what happened afterward?

- Compare two approaches you've used—peer feedback vs. teacher feedback—for supporting collaboration online. What strengths did each bring, and how might you combine them?

- In groups, draft one "class change" you could implement next week based on a likely pattern in your setting (e.g., re-entry after tech glitches, uneven participation in breakout rooms). Outline how you'll explain the change to students and how you'll know it helped.

Chapter 10: Future Directions for SEL in Digital Learning

Introduction

As we look ahead, it's clear that social and emotional learning will not sit on the sidelines of digital education—it will shape how we teach, learn, and relate to one another online. New tools are arriving rapidly, but the heart of the work remains the same: helping students recognize their emotions, steady themselves when it's challenging, understand others' perspectives, and act with care in shared spaces.

What changes is the setting. More growth now happens through screens, platforms, and blended routines stretching across home and school.

This shift asks all of us—teachers, families, school leaders, and students—to stay flexible. A new app can change the rhythm of a class; an updated platform can alter how feedback lands; a message posted in the wrong tone can echo farther and faster than a hallway comment ever would.

When we treat SEL as part of the digital environment itself, not an add-on, we help students carry their skills from chat to video to collaborative docs without losing the thread of dignity, agency, and belonging.

We also know the stakes. The skills that let young people navigate complexity—adapting to change, collaborating across distance, making ethical choices with data and devices—are the same skills employers and communities say they need most in the coming decade.

Global guidance[100] on the future of education points in that direction, emphasizing competencies like self-regulation, collaboration, and responsible decision-making alongside academics. And as technologies like artificial intelligence find their way into everyday classroom workflows, the need for human judgment grows, not shrinks. Educators will be asked to pair powerful tools with clear guardrails, and students will need practical ways to check bias, protect privacy, and use assistance ethically—work that fits squarely within SEL's scope.

This chapter stays close to the classroom while looking forward. We'll explore how emerging technologies might support or strain social-emotional growth, why adaptability and lifelong learning belong at the center of SEL in digital spaces, and what a humane, future-facing vision could look like when schools, families, and communities move together. The aim is simple: keep what is deeply human at the core, and use technology to widen—not narrow—the circle of care.

Emerging Technologies Influencing SEL

New tools won't replace the human heart of SEL, but they can widen our reach. When used carefully, technology can help us notice students who need support, create safe practice

---

[100] Organisation for Economic Co-operation and Development. (n.d.). Future of education and skills 2030 (Education and Skills Policy Programme). OECD. https://www.oecd.org/en/about/projects/future-of-education-and-skills-2030.html

spaces for empathy, and keep families and teachers moving in the same direction. The notes below focus on what each technology can realistically add—and the guardrails that keep student dignity front and center.

1. Artificial Intelligence (AI)

AI can personalize support by surfacing just-in-time prompts, study plans, or check-ins that match a student's emotional and academic status. The promise is paired with clear cautions: transparency, bias checks, and strong data protections. International guidance[101] stresses exactly that balance: use AI to extend teaching, not replace relationships; keep humans in the loop; and make uses explainable to students and families.

Why it matters for SEL: AI can nudge reflection ("name one feeling, name one next step"), suggest adaptive practice after a setback, and flag when a learner might benefit from a human check-in—always with clear consent and teacher oversight.

2. Virtual Reality (VR) and Augmented Reality (AR)

Immersive scenarios can help students try to see things from another point of view without social risk. VR, in particular, has shown the potential to strengthen empathic responding beyond the headset session when experiences are well designed and followed by reflection—evidence from

---

[101] Organisation for Economic Co-operation and Development. (2023). *OECD Digital Education Outlook 2023: Emerging governance of generative AI in education* [Chapter 10]. OECD Publishing. https://doi.org/10.1787/c74f03de-en

controlled studies[102] points to measurable, longer-term gains in perspective-taking and prosocial attitudes.

Why it matters for SEL: A guided VR moment—say, navigating school as a newcomer—can make abstract discussions about inclusion concrete. The debrief is the key: students need space to process what they felt and what they might do differently next time.

3. Gamification

Game elements—clear goals, immediate feedback, visible progress—can make SEL routines stick. Points or badges are optional; the real engine is designed to reward collaboration, persistence after failure, and respectful communication.

Short, replayable challenges that ask students to plan, try, review, and try again mirror the habits we want in daily classwork.

Why it matters for SEL: When effort and prosocial choices unlock progress, students experience the core message of growth mindset and teamwork, rather than just hearing it.

4. Social Media and Online Communities

Private class spaces and moderated groups can extend belonging beyond the live session. Students can share strategies that helped them manage stress, give credit for ideas, and practice civil disagreement in writing.

---

[102] Herrera, F., Bailenson, J., Weisz, E., Ogle, E., & Zaki, J. (2018). *Building long-term empathy: A large-scale comparison of traditional and virtual-reality perspective-taking.* PLOS ONE, 13(10), e0204494. https://doi.org/10.1371/journal.pone.0204494

The non-negotiables are privacy[103], consent, and clarity about what is never posted. Practical checklists from neutral experts help schools set those boundaries in plain language.

Why it matters for SEL: When norms are visible and modeled by adults, online spaces can become practice grounds for empathy, perspective-taking, and repair after misreads.

5. Data Analytics

Light-touch, ethical data use can help you notice patterns— who is engaging, who might be withdrawing, and which routines seem to lower stress. The purpose is support, not labels.

Think small and transparent. Before you collect anything, tell students and families what you'll look at (for example: attendance in live sessions, number of posts, a one-word mood check), why it matters, how it will be stored (within district tools), and how long you'll keep it. Keep options open—allow anonymous check-ins, offer an opt-out, and never tie SEL-related responses to grades. Aim for the minimum useful information: counts and trends, not detailed dossiers.

A few gentle signals are usually enough: participation over time, response rates to quick polls, on-task time during a focused work block, or the proportion of students who submit a brief "next step" after feedback. Look for direction, not perfection. If breakout-room talk dips after 20 minutes, shorten the window and add simple roles; if a Monday mood

---

[103] Common Sense Privacy Program. (n.d.). *Common Sense Privacy: Protecting kids' privacy in a digital world.* https://privacy.commonsense.org/

check trends "tired," start class with a shorter warm-up; if three students go quiet in forums, invite them to reply by audio instead of text.

Close the loop. Share back what you're seeing ("Many of us felt rushed on quizzes; we're adding a two-minute preview") and what you'll try next. Keep reflections voluntary and brief, and delete raw responses on a regular schedule. When students see that small bits of information lead to visible care—clearer routines, more flexible ways to participate—their trust grows along with your ability to support them.

Why it matters for SEL: Used this way, data becomes a mirror, not a microscope. It helps you make humane, everyday adjustments—tweaking check-ins, rebalancing groups, revisiting norms—while protecting dignity and privacy.

The Importance of Adaptability and Lifelong Learning in the Context of SEL

Change isn't a visitor in our classrooms—it lives there. New tools roll in, schedules shift, family circumstances evolve, and the world outside the window keeps moving. When we treat adaptability and lifelong learning as part of social and emotional learning, we give students—and ourselves—a steadier way to meet that motion.

Adaptability is how we flex without breaking; lifelong learning is how we keep growing on purpose. Together, they make daily challenges feel manageable and turn surprises into opportunities for practice rather than panic.

1. Embracing Change

Students watch how we respond when plans wobble: the platform glitches, a deadline needs adjusting, or a discussion veers off course. If we name what changed, keep expectations kind and clear, and invite the class to re-center, we model resilience in real time. In digital spaces, small rituals help—brief "here's what's new, here's what's the same" openers, a one-minute reset after a tech snag, and a predictable way to ask for help.

Over time, students learn that uncertainty isn't a failure state; it's a moment to breathe, ask a question, and try the next step. That stance lowers anxiety and keeps attention on the learning rather than the disruption.

2. Lifelong Learning and SEL

Lifelong learning is less a program than a posture: we stay curious, seek feedback, and treat skill as something we can build. SEL makes that posture concrete. A student who can say, "I didn't understand that yet—can I try another example?" is already practicing self-awareness, self-advocacy, and healthy persistence.

You can nurture this with short, regular routines: reflective exit prompts ("What helped you move forward today?"), opportunities to revise work after feedback and choose a challenge that feels just above comfortable.

These habits[104] teach students that growth doesn't end with a grade—it rides along with them, class to class and year to year.

---

[104] American Psychological Association. (n.d.). *Resilience.*
https://www.apa.org/topics/resilience/building-your-resilience

3. Adapting SEL Practices

As tools and contexts change, our SEL moves should travel with us without becoming heavy. Keep the core steady—belonging, voice, clear norms—and update the surface. If your class shifts platforms, translate your norms into the new space (how to ask for a turn, how to credit ideas, where to find help). If student feedback shows that check-ins feel repetitive, try a different format (a one-word mood slider one week, a "first step after feedback" note the next).

If access changes for some families, widen the door—offer text as well as email, audio as well as written posts, and wider windows for participation. [105]Professional learning matters here, too: brief, hands-on sessions where teachers test a routine, watch a colleague model it, and leave with a template they can use tomorrow.

In practice, this section boils down to a few promises we keep with students: we will tell you what's changing, keep routines humane and predictable, and give you ways to grow that make sense for you. When classrooms keep those promises—online or in person—young people learn to meet change with steadiness and keep learning long after the assignment ends.

---

[105] Organisation for Economic Co-operation and Development. (2019). *Skills for 2030: Concept note* (OECD Future of Education and Skills 2030). OECD. https://www.oecd.org/content/dam/oecd/en/about/projects/edu/education-2040/concept-notes/Skills_for_2030_concept_note.pdf

A Vision for the Future of SEL in Education

The picture ahead is less about adding a new initiative and more about weaving SEL into how learning feels—online and in person. When classrooms share a common language for emotions, families and community partners echo that language, and when technology is used to widen access rather than add noise, students experience school as a place that steadies and stretches them.

1. Holistic integration across subjects

SEL belongs inside everyday lessons, not beside them. In math, students can narrate how they reasoned together before showing the final answer. In science, groups can plan a "reset routine" for when an experiment fails—thirty quiet seconds, then one sentence naming the next step. In literature, peer feedback can be anchored to three cues: name the strength, ask a clarifying question, and suggest one change.

Over time, these small moves create a classroom where thinking hard and treating people well are the same job. What this looks like for teachers: you build two or three SEL habits into the flow—opening check-ins with plain feeling words, a shared decision rule for groups, and a closing reflection that asks, "What helped you persist today?" Because the routines repeat across subjects, students don't have to re-learn expectations; they can spend their energy on the work.

2. Shared work with families and the community

Students do better when the language at home and school matches. Families don't need a binder; they need a sentence or two that shows what you're practicing and how to try it at home. A weekly note—"We're practicing asking for help early; try 'What's your first step?' at dinner"—travels further than a long newsletter. Community partners can help carry the message: a counselor co-hosts a 15-minute evening demo on calm homework routines; the local library keeps one-page "how we repair after conflict" cards at the desk.

Practical anchors: one primary communication channel (so families aren't chasing messages), translation where possible, and flexible office hours (an early morning option helps shift workers). Invite families to tell you what already works for their child and fold those ideas into class routines. That reciprocity builds trust and makes support feel shared rather than assigned.

3. Culturally responsive, identity-affirming practice

SEL has power when it reflects who students are. That means examples, texts, scenarios that mirror students' languages, histories, and communities—and space for students to choose how to participate. Offer options: a brief audio response or a written post; camera on or thoughtful chat; individual draft or paired outline. Invite students to co-write discussion norms and to lead a warm-up or closure once a month.

Why this matters in daily life: belonging grows when students see themselves in the work and have a real say in how it runs. It also lowers the emotional cost of participating online, where tone can be misread and confidence can dip. When identity is honored, feedback lands as partnership, not judgment.

4. Every day mental-health promotion

Well-being shouldn't appear only when something goes wrong. Build it into transitions: a 60-second breathing cue before a hard task, a quick "name one feeling, name one next step" after feedback, a visible map of where to seek help (teacher, counselor, peer mentor). Keep privacy clear—no one has to disclose; participation can be quiet.

Global health guidance[106] underscores the value of promotive and preventive supports in school settings and the importance of safeguarding students' dignity while doing so.

In practice: you keep routines brief and predictable, you explain the "why" in plain language, and you make opting in easy (a reaction emoji counts). The goal isn't to fix feelings; it's to give students a few steady ways to return to thinking when the moment is turbulent.

5. Technology that simplifies human work

Use tools that make connections easier, not heavier. A single "home base" platform cuts confusion. Short polls can surface class climate ("I felt heard today: 1–5") and guide one small change tomorrow. Discussion boards work best with tight prompts and clear reply norms ("credit the idea you're building on; ask one question before you disagree").

---

[106] World Health Organization. (2020). *Guidelines on mental health promotive and preventive interventions for adolescents: Helping adolescents thrive* [PDF]. https://www.who.int/publications/i/item/9789240011854

Simulations and role-play—whether low-tech scenarios or richer digital experiences—let students practice perspective-taking and ethical decisions safely.

Keep the stance: low-stakes, formative, transparent. Students should always know how information will be used (to tune routines, not to sort people). Tech supports the rhythm you already run: open with a check-in, give structured collaboration, close with a reflection and a preview of what you'll adjust based on what you learned from them.

6. A wider horizon: local care to global responsibility

SEL matures when students use it beyond the classroom. Link projects to real issues that students care about—such as water quality on their block, accessibility at nearby shops, food security in the neighborhood, or climate resilience in their city. Ask groups to gather multiple perspectives, propose a small, doable action, and reflect on how collaboration changed their view.

Day-to-day texture: a class might interview two community members, draft a brief "what we learned" post for the school site, and present a one-page plan to a partner organization. Students experience empathy as contribution—not just understanding others, but working with them to make something better.

Putting it all together

Keep SEL inside the lesson, share language with families, honor identity, make well-being preventive, let technology clarify rather than complicate, and connect learning to real problems students can touch. Do it through small, repeatable moves. When those moves are steady, students lean into hard work with more trust and stamina—and the culture you're building can flex with whatever comes next.

The Potential Impact of SEL on Society

When social and emotional learning becomes part of daily practice—not a one-off lesson—its effects reach beyond a single classroom. The habits students build together—listening well, naming feelings, repairing conflict, and acting with care—shape how they show up in families, workplaces, neighborhoods, and the wider world. The points below retain your original framing; only the links are updated, and a brief introduction is included.

1. Creating Empathetic Leaders

When students practice perspective-taking, constructive feedback, and ethical decision-making every day, those habits follow them into internships, workplaces, and public life. Teams run by people who listen well and respond with care tend to collaborate more smoothly and innovate more consistently.

Global workforce analyses now list social and emotional capacities—like collaboration, empathy, and communication—among the skills that enable effective leadership in complex settings, a signal that what we teach in class can ripple outward into healthier organizations and communities.

2. Reducing Mental Health Issues

Schools that make space for naming feelings, asking for help, and repairing conflict send a powerful message: seeking support is normal. That climate lowers the threshold for early intervention and gives students practical tools—breathing, reframing, planning a next step—before stress hardens into crisis.

Public health guidance[107] identifies social connection and supportive school climates as protective factors linked with better mental health and reduced risk of anxiety and depression, underscoring SEL's contribution to population-level well-being.

3. Promoting Equity and Inclusion

SEL that is culturally responsive helps every student see their identity respected and their voice welcomed. When classroom norms invite multiple ways to participate, when curriculum includes many stories and histories, and when students help shape rules and routines, participation widens and gaps narrow.

Frameworks[108] that center assets, context, and student agency give schools practical ways to align SEL with equity so belonging isn't accidental—it's designed.

---

[107] Office of the Surgeon General. (2023, May 3). *Our epidemic of loneliness and isolation: The U.S. Surgeon General's Advisory on the healing effects of social connection and community* [PDF]. U.S. Department of Health and Human Services. https://www.hhs.gov/surgeongeneral/reports-and-publications/connection/index.html

[108] Collaborative for Academic, Social, and Emotional Learning (CASEL). (n.d.). *How does social and emotional learning (SEL) support educational equity and*

4. Strengthening Communities

Relationships are the threads that hold communities together. Students who learn how to express care, challenge one another to grow, share power, and extend support bring those habits to clubs, workplaces, and neighborhood projects.

Local initiatives—from peer mentoring to youth advisory boards—thrive when young people[109] have practiced these "relational muscles," creating a feedback loop in which strong ties make collective problem-solving possible.

5. Enhancing Global Cooperation

Today's problems cross borders; so must our capacity for empathy and dialogue. When learners engage with perspectives beyond their own—through language exchanges, collaborative projects, or case studies of global challenges—they practice listening across difference and acting with a sense of shared responsibility.

Global competence frameworks[110] place these capacities at the center, preparing young people to work with others on issues like health, climate, and human rights.

These impacts build on one another. A student who feels connected is more likely to ask for help; a classroom that

---

excellence? https://casel.org/fundamentals-of-sel/how-does-sel-support-educational-equity-and-excellence/transformative-sel/

[109] Search Institute. (n.d.). *Developmental relationships: Relationships to help young people thrive.* https://searchinstitute.org/developmental-relationships

[110] Organisation for Economic Co-operation and Development. (2018). *Handbook PISA 2018: Global competence.*
https://www.oecd.org/content/dam/oecd/en/topics/policy-sub-issues/global-competence/Handbook-PISA-2018-Global-Competence.pdf

welcomes many voices becomes a school where fair processes are normal; a school that partners with families and community sends graduates into the world ready to lead with empathy. That is how daily SEL routines grow into a healthier society.

Conclusion

The future of SEL in digital learning will be shaped by the everyday choices we make—how we greet students in an online classroom, which routines we maintain, when we pause to teach repair, and how we utilize new tools without losing sight of human needs. As technology evolves, our guiding principle remains unchanged: students learn best when they feel safe, seen, and capable of growth.

This chapter sets out a path: invite thoughtful uses of AI, VR/AR, games, online communities, and light-touch data; keep adaptability and lifelong learning at the center; and build a schoolwide vision where SEL is woven through subjects, grounded in culture and equity, and supported by families and community partners. None of this requires perfection. It asks for clarity of purpose, small, consistent moves, and a willingness to revise as we learn.

The journey is ongoing. When educators, families, and community organizations pull in the same direction, students carry the same steady message across platforms and places: your feelings are workable, effort changes outcomes, and we are in this with you. That is the kind of coherence that helps young people thrive—academically, emotionally, and as citizens of an interconnected world.

Reflection Questions

- Where, in your current digital routines, do students most clearly experience belonging—and where does that feeling thin out?

- Which one SEL practice from this chapter could you start next week with minimal prep (e.g., a two-minute check-in, a clearer repair routine, or a short student reflection)?

- What data do you actually need to guide SEL decisions (patterns, not profiles), and how will you communicate to students how that information is used?

- How will you make your SEL approach more culturally responsive—whose voices, languages, and examples will you add?

- What will you stop doing to make room for a steadier, simpler SEL routine?

Discussion Prompts

- Share one emerging technology (AI tutor, VR scenario, game mechanic, or simple analytics view) you could try in your class. What *human* goal would it serve (belonging, repair, focus), and how will you keep it optional and low-stakes?

- Draft two sentences you'd use to explain an SEL-aligned tech routine to families in plain language. How will you name the benefits, risks, and the opt-out?

- Think of a recent change you made (new norm, new tool, new schedule). What evidence—student voice, brief check-ins, work samples—told you it helped or needed revision?

- In pairs, sketch a one-week mini-unit where an academic goal and an SEL goal travel together (e.g., argument writing + perspective-taking). Where will reflection or repair show up?

- Identify one equity risk of a tool you use (bandwidth, language access, privacy, sensory load). What's a concrete adjustment that widens access without lowering expectations?

- Write a 30-second "future vision" message to students: how you'll keep class human as tools change. Read it aloud. What wording felt most honest and steady?

- Map your partners (counselor, librarian, community org, student leaders). What is one small collaboration you can set up this month to support SEL beyond your classroom?

- Choose one mindset to model publicly next week—adaptability, curiosity, or repair. What specific moment will you narrate ("Here's what I'll try; here's how I'll adjust if it doesn't work")?

Glossary of Key Terms

SEL Basics

- ### Social and Emotional Learning (SEL)

The process of learning to understand and manage emotions, build healthy relationships, and make responsible choices.

Example: Practicing how to apologize and repair after hurting someone's feelings.

- ### SEL Competencies

The core skill areas SEL develops are self-awareness, self-management, social awareness, relationship skills, and responsible decision-making.

Example: Calming yourself when angry and contributing fairly in a team.

- ### Self-Awareness

Recognizing your emotions, thoughts, and strengths—and how they influence behavior.

Example: Noticing you feel nervous before a test and naming it.

- ### Self-Management

Regulating emotions, thoughts, and behaviors in different situations.

Example: Using a breathing strategy to stay calm when homework is frustrating.

- **Social Awareness**

Understanding others' perspectives and needs; showing empathy and respect.

Example: Seeing a classmate who is down and asking if they want to talk.

- **Relationship Skills**

Communicating clearly, listening actively, cooperating, and navigating conflict.

Example: Listening without interrupting and sharing ideas constructively in a group.

- **Responsible Decision-Making**

Making caring, ethical choices for yourself and others.

Example: Choosing to finish homework before gaming.

Emotional Skills and Well-being

- **Emotional Literacy**

Identifying emotions and talking about them with accurate language.

Example: Saying "I feel angry" or "I'm excited," instead of "I don't know."

- **Emotional Regulation**

Managing intensity and duration of feelings so they support learning and relationships.

Example: Counting to ten when you're mad instead of yelling.

- **Emotional Well-Being**

A general sense of calm, confidence, and capacity to cope with stress.

Example: Feeling steady even with a big test ahead.

- **Emotional Check-In**

A quick practice to notice and share your current mood.

Example: Selecting a mood icon at the start of class.

- **Emotional Overload**

Feeling overwhelmed by several strong emotions at once.

Example: Stress and sadness are piling up due to heavy workloads and worries.

- **Self-Compassion**

Responding to your own mistakes with kindness and a plan to try again.

Example: Telling yourself, "It's okay—next time I'll start earlier."

Digital Learning and Technology

- **Digital Classroom**

A learning setting that uses devices and online platforms for instruction.

Example: Attending a live lesson on a video-conferencing app.

- **Digital Distractions**

On-screen alerts, apps, or sites that pull attention away from learning.

Example: Checking messages during a reading assignment.

- **Digital Literacy**

Using technology safely, effectively, and thoughtfully.

Example: Evaluating websites for credible information and avoiding scams.

- **Digital Tools**

Apps, websites, and software that support learning and communication.

Example: Collaborating in Google Docs on a shared report.

- **Digital Storytelling**

Using multimedia (images, audio, video) to share ideas or experiences.

Example: Creating a short video about a favorite hobby.

- **Digital Citizenship**

Acting safely, respectfully, and responsibly online.

Example: Protecting personal information and being kind in comments.

- **Responsible Technology Use**

Setting healthy tech habits and boundaries.

Example: Not clicking on unknown links and asking an adult when unsure.

- **Virtual Learning Environment (VLE)**

The online space where course materials, assignments, and interactions live.

Example: Working in Google Classroom to access lessons and submit work.

- **Virtual Support Circles**

Online groups that share feelings and offer peer support.

Example: A weekly video check-in where classmates talk about how they're doing.

- **Virtual Parent–Teacher Conferences**

Meetings held via video to discuss progress and well-being.

Example: A Zoom conference to review goals and supports.

Learning Skills and Strategies

- **Assessment Tools**

Methods for gauging social-emotional growth and needs.

Example: A brief survey about how you manage frustration.

- **Self-Assessment**

Reflecting on your progress and identifying next steps.

Example: "I'm strong in reading; I'll practice spelling 10 minutes daily."

- **Reflection**

Looking back on an experience to learn from it.

Example: After a project, note what worked and what to try differently.

- **Reflection Journals**

Written entries about thoughts, feelings, and learning.

Example: Recording a weekly "high, low, next step."

- **Goal Setting**

Choosing a clear target and a plan for reaching it.

Example: Reading one book per week and tracking pages daily.

- **Mindfulness**

Paying gentle attention to the present moment.

Example: Noticing your breath for one minute before starting work.

- **Mindfulness Apps**

Mobile tools that guide calm focus and relaxation.

Example: Using an app for a two-minute breathing exercise.

- **Time Management Techniques**

Organizing tasks and time to reduce stress and finish work.

Example: Scheduling 25-minute focus blocks with 5-minute breaks.

- **Engagement**

Active participation and attention in learning.

Example: Posting in the discussion and contributing to a group task.

- **Motivation**

The drive to begin, persist, and improve.

Example: Working toward a personal goal because the topic matters to you.

Social Skills and Relationships

- **Collaboration**

Working with others toward a shared goal.

Example: Dividing roles and creating a poster together.

- **Peer Mentoring**

Guidance from a more experienced student to a less experienced peer.

Example: An older student helping a newcomer learn class routines.

- **Peer Feedback**

Specific comments from classmates to help improve work.

Example: "Your examples are clear; consider adding a counterpoint."

- **Peer Support**

Encouragement and help among students.

Example: A friend checks in when you're stuck and studies with you.

- **Active Listening**

Giving full attention and showing understanding.

Example: Facing the speaker, nodding, and summarizing what you heard.

- **Conflict Resolution**

Solving disagreements respectfully and fairly.

Example: Naming the problem, sharing perspectives, and agreeing on a plan.

Mental Health and Well-Being

- **Mental Health**

Emotional and psychological functioning that supports daily life.

Example: Managing stress and enjoying activities with others.

- **Resilience**

Recovering and learning after setbacks.

Example: Trying again after a poor quiz and improving the next time.

- **Stress Management**

Strategies to reduce pressure and regain focus.

Example: Taking a short walk and resetting before returning to work.

- **Supportive Peer Interactions**

Positive, caring exchanges that help classmates cope and grow.

Example: Listening to a friend's tough day and checking in later.

School and Community

- **Inclusive Environment**

A setting where everyone feels safe, seen, and valued.

Example: Ensuring all voices are invited into discussions.

- **Cultural Responsiveness**

Respecting and integrating diverse identities and traditions.

Example: Including texts and examples that reflect students' cultures.

- **Social-Issue Awareness Campaigns**

Efforts to inform and mobilize others around community needs.

Example: Creating posters and posts about recycling or mental-health supports.

- **Community Engagement**

Learning with—and contributing to—your local community.

Example: Volunteering at a neighborhood clean-up.

- **Student Leadership**

Students shaping activities, culture, and solutions.

Example: Organizing a peer-mentoring club or wellness day.

References

Albulescu, P., Macsinga, I., Rusu, A., Sulea, C., Bodnaru, A., & Tulbure, B. T. (2022). "Give me a break!" A systematic review and meta-analysis on the efficacy of micro-breaks for increasing well-being and performance. *PLOS ONE, 17*(8), e0272460. https://doi.org/10.1371/journal.pone.0272460

American Academy of Pediatrics. (n.d.). *How to make a family media use plan.* HealthyChildren.org. https://www.healthychildren.org/English/family-life/Media/Pages/How-to-Make-a-Family-Media-Use-Plan.aspx

American Psychological Association. (2023, May). *Health advisory on social media use in adolescence* [PDF]. https://www.apa.org/topics/social-media-internet/health-advisory-adolescent-social-media-use.pdf

American Psychological Association. (n.d.). *Resilience.* https://www.apa.org/topics/resilience/building-your-resilience

Andrade, H. (2019). A critical review of research on student self-assessment. *Frontiers in Education, 4*, 87. https://doi.org/10.3389/feduc.2019.00087

Andrade, H., & Valtcheva, A. (2009). Promoting learning and achievement through self-assessment. *Theory Into Practice, 48*(1), 12–19. https://doi.org/10.1080/00405840802577544

Black, P., & Wiliam, D. (1998). Inside the black box: Raising standards through classroom assessment. *Phi Delta*

Kappan, 80(2), 139–148. https://www.michigan.gov/-/media/Project/Websites/mde/2017/09/18/Inside_The_Black_Box_-_Black_and_William.pdf?rev=da79805095b64f1881d473deac26acd2

Center on the Developing Child at Harvard University. (n.d.). *Serve and return: Back-and-forth exchanges.* https://developingchild.harvard.edu/key-concept/serve-and-return/

Centers for Disease Control and Prevention. (2024, December 3). *Enhance connectedness among students, staff, and families.* https://www.cdc.gov/mental-health-action-guide/strategies/enhance-connectedness.html

Claro, S., Paunesku, D., & Dweck, C. S. (2016). Growth mindset tempers the effects of poverty on academic achievement. *Proceedings of the National Academy of Sciences of the United States of America, 113*(31), 8664–8668. https://doi.org/10.1073/pnas.1608207113

Collaborative for Academic, Social, and Emotional Learning (CASEL). (n.d.). *Assessment tools.* https://casel.org/state-resource-center/assessment-tools

Collaborative for Academic, Social, and Emotional Learning (CASEL). (n.d.). *Family partnerships.* CASEL. https://schoolguide.casel.org/focus-area-3/family-partnerships/

Collaborative for Academic, Social, and Emotional Learning (CASEL). (n.d.). *How does social and emotional learning*

(SEL) support educational equity and excellence?
https://casel.org/fundamentals-of-sel/how-does-sel-support-educational-equity-and-excellence/transformative-sel/

Common Sense Education. (n.d.). *Keeping your students (and yourself) safe on social media: A checklist.*
https://www.commonsense.org/education/articles/keeping-your-students-and-yourself-safe-on-social-media-a-checklist

Common Sense Privacy Program. (n.d.). *Common Sense Privacy: Protecting kids' privacy in a digital world.*
https://privacy.commonsense.org/

Drew, A. L., Hill, A., & Whitmire, K. (2024). What do parents know about social-emotional learning in their children's schools? Gaps and opportunities for strengthening intervention impact. *Heliyon, 10,* Article e2400391.
https://www.sciencedirect.com/science/article/pii/S2773233924000391

Dunlosky, J., Rawson, K. A., Marsh, E. J., Nathan, M. J., & Willingham, D. T. (2013). Improving students' learning with effective learning techniques: Promising directions from cognitive and educational psychology. *Psychological Science in the Public Interest, 14*(1), 4–58.
https://doi.org/10.1177/1529100612453266

Dweck, C. S. (2016). *Mindset: The new psychology of success* (Updated ed.). Random House Publishing Group.
https://www.penguinrandomhouse.com/books/44330/mindset-by-carol-s-dweck-phd/

Education Endowment Foundation. (2018). *Working with parents to support children's learning: Guidance report*. Education Endowment Foundation. https://d2tic4wvo1iusb.cloudfront.net/production/eef-guidance-reports/supporting-parents/EEF_Parental_Engagement_Guidance_Report.pdf

Faverio, M., Anderson, M., & Park, E. (2025, April 22). *Teens, social media, and mental health*. Pew Research Center. https://www.pewresearch.org/internet/2025/04/22/teens-social-media-and-mental-health/

Gehlbach, H., & Hough, H. J. (2018, May). *Measuring social emotional learning through student surveys in the CORE districts: A pragmatic approach to validity and reliability* [Report]. Policy Analysis for California Education. https://edpolicyinca.org/publications/measuring-social-emotional-learning-through-student-surveys-core-districts

Herrera, F., Bailenson, J., Weisz, E., Ogle, E., & Zaki, J. (2018). Building long-term empathy: A large-scale comparison of traditional and virtual-reality perspective-taking. *PLOS ONE, 13*(10), e0204494. https://doi.org/10.1371/journal.pone.0204494

Hattie, J., & Timperley, H. (2007). The power of feedback. *Review of Educational Research, 77*(1), 81–112. https://doi.org/10.3102/003465430298487

Kraft, M. A., & Rogers, T. (2015). The underutilized potential of teacher-to-parent communication: Evidence from a field experiment. *Economics of Education Review, 47*, 49–63. https://doi.org/10.1016/j.econedurev.2015.04.001

Kruger, J., Epley, N., Parker, J., & Ng, Z. W. (2005). Egocentrism over e-mail: Can people communicate as well as they think? *Journal of Personality and Social Psychology, 89*(6), 925–936. https://web-docs.stern.nyu.edu/pa/kruger_email_ego.pdf

Lawson, G. M., McKenzie, M. E., Becker, K. D., Selby, L., & Hoover, S. A. (2019). The core components of evidence-based social and emotional learning (SEL) programs. *Prevention Science, 20*(4), 457–467. https://doi.org/10.1007/s11121-018-0953-y

Leech, N. L., Gullett, S., Cummings, M. H., & Haug, C. A. (2022). The challenges of remote K–12 education during the COVID-19 pandemic: Differences by grade level. *Online Learning, 26*(1), 245–267. https://doi.org/10.24059/olj.v26i1.2609

Locke, E. A., & Latham, G. P. (2002). Building a practically useful theory of goal setting and task motivation: A 35-year odyssey. *American Psychologist, 57*(9), 705–717. https://doi.org/10.1037/0003-066X.57.9.705

Masten, A. S. (2001). *Ordinary magic: Resilience processes in development* [PDF]. https://ocfcpacourts.us/wp-content/uploads/2020/06/Ordinary_Magic_Resilience_Process_000935.pdf

Martínez-Yarza, N., Solabarrieta-Eizaguirre, J., & Santibáñez-Gruber, R. (2024). The impact of family involvement on students' social-emotional development: The mediational role of school engagement. *European Journal of*

Psychology of Education, 39(4), 4297–4327.
https://doi.org/10.1007/s10212-024-00862-1

National PTA. (n.d.). *Family-school partnerships.*
https://www.pta.org/home/run-your-pta/family-school-partnerships

National PTA. (n.d.). *Standard 6—Collaborating with community: Assessment guide.*
https://www.pta.org/docs/default-source/files/programs/national-standards-for-family-school-partnerships/assessment_guide_standard_6.pdf

Nicol, D. J., & Macfarlane-Dick, D. (2006). Formative assessment and self-regulated learning: A model and seven principles of good feedback practice. *Studies in Higher Education, 31*(2), 199–218.
https://doi.org/10.1080/03075070600572090

Nixon, C. L. (2014). Current perspectives: The impact of cyberbullying on adolescent health. *Adolescent Health, Medicine and Therapeutics, 5*, 143–158.
https://doi.org/10.2147/AHMT.S36456
https://www.ncbi.nlm.nih.gov/pmc/articles/PMC4126576/

OECD. (2024). *Social and emotional skills for better lives: Findings from the OECD Survey on Social and Emotional Skills 2023.* OECD Publishing. https://doi.org/10.1787/35ca7b7c-en

Office of the Surgeon General. (2023, May 3). *Our epidemic of loneliness and isolation: The U.S. Surgeon General's Advisory on the healing effects of social connection and community* [PDF]. U.S.

Department of Health and Human Services.
https://www.hhs.gov/surgeongeneral/reports-and-
publications/connection/index.html

Organisation for Economic Co-operation and
Development. (n.d.). *Future of education and skills 2030
(Education and Skills Policy Programme)*. OECD.
https://www.oecd.org/en/about/projects/future-of-
education-and-skills-2030.html

Organisation for Economic Co-operation and
Development. (2018). *Handbook PISA 2018: Global competence.*
https://www.oecd.org/content/dam/oecd/en/topics/policy
-sub-issues/global-competence/Handbook-PISA-2018-
Global-Competence.pdf

Organisation for Economic Co-operation and
Development. (2019). *Skills for 2030: Concept note (OECD
Future of Education and Skills 2030)*. OECD.
https://www.oecd.org/content/dam/oecd/en/about/projec
ts/edu/education-2040/concept-
notes/Skills_for_2030_concept_note.pdf

Organisation for Economic Co-operation and
Development. (2023). *OECD Digital Education Outlook 2023:
Emerging governance of generative AI in education* [Chapter 10].
OECD Publishing. https://doi.org/10.1787/c74f03de-en

Paunesku, D., Walton, G. M., Romero, C., Smith, E. N.,
Yeager, D. S., & Dweck, C. S. (2015). Mind-set interventions
are a scalable treatment for academic underachievement.
Psychological Science, 26(6), 784–793.
https://doi.org/10.1177/0956797615571017

Patchin, J. W., & Hinduja, S. (2024). *2023 Cyberbullying Data*. Cyberbullying Research Center. Retrieved October 20, 2025, from https://cyberbullying.org/2023-cyberbullying-data

Pettigrew, T. F., & Tropp, L. R. (2008). How does intergroup contact reduce prejudice? Meta-analytic tests of three mediators. *European Journal of Social Psychology, 38*(6), 922–934. https://doi.org/10.1002/ejsp.504

Phan, M. L., Renshaw, T. L., Caramanico, J., Greeson, J. M., MacKenzie, E., Atkinson-Diaz, Z., Doppelt, N., Tai, H., Mandell, D. S., & Nuske, H. J. (2022). Mindfulness-based school interventions: A systematic review of outcome evidence quality by study design. *Mindfulness, 13*(7), 1591–1613. https://doi.org/10.1007/s12671-022-01885-9

Quigley, A., Muijs, D., & Stringer, E. (2018, April 27). *Metacognition and self-regulated learning: Guidance report.* Education Endowment Foundation. https://educationendowmentfoundation.org.uk/education-evidence/guidance-reports/metacognition

Raposa, E. B., Rhodes, J. E., Stams, G. J. M., Card, N., Burton, S., Schwartz, S. E. O., Sykes, L. A. Y., Kanchewa, S., Kupersmidt, J., & Hussain, S. (2019). The effects of youth mentoring programs: A meta-analysis of outcome studies. *Journal of Youth and Adolescence, 48*(3), 423–443. https://doi.org/10.1007/s10964-019-00982-8

Rawson, R., & Rhodes, C. (2022). Peer-Assisted Learning Online: Peer leader motivations and experiences. *Journal of Peer Learning, 15,* 32–47.

https://journalofpeerlearning.org/articles/105/files/66951d9
0e5743.pdf

Richards, D., & Viganó, N. (2019). *Digital technology and teacher stress: Impact of school conditions and the role of coping strategies* [Unpublished manuscript]. Queen's University Belfast. https://pureadmin.qub.ac.uk/ws/portalfiles/portal/1479264
61/3013046.pdf

Roseth, C. J., Johnson, D. W., & Johnson, R. T. (2008). Promoting early adolescents' achievement and peer relationships: The effects of cooperative, competitive, and individualistic goal structures. *Psychological Bulletin, 134*(2), 223–246. https://doi.org/10.1037/0033-2909.134.2.223

Schneider, B. (2003, March 1). Trust in schools: A core resource for school reform. *ASCD*. https://www.ascd.org/el/articles/trust-in-schools-a-core-resource-for-school-reform

Search Institute. (2018). *Developmental Relationships Framework*. https://www.search-institute.org/wp-content/uploads/2018/05/Developmental-Relationships-Framework_English.pdf

Search Institute. (n.d.). *Developmental relationships: Relationships to help young people thrive.* https://searchinstitute.org/developmental-relationships

Sheridan, S. M., Kim, E. M., Coutts, M. J., Sjuts, T. M., Holmes, S. R., Ransom, K. A., & Garbacz, S. A. (2012). *Clarifying parent involvement and family-school partnership intervention research: A preliminary synthesis (CYFS Working Paper No. 2012-4)*

[PDF]. Nebraska Center for Research on Children, Youth, Families & Schools (CYFS), University of Nebraska–Lincoln. https://www.cyfs.unl.edu/resources/downloads/working-papers/CYFS_Working_Paper_2012_4.pdf

Sheridan, S. M., Knoche, L. L., Edwards, C. P., Bovaird, B., & Kupzyk, K. A. (2010). Parent engagement and school readiness: Effects of the Getting Ready intervention on preschool children's social-emotional competencies. *Early Education and Development, 21*(1), 125–156. https://www.ncbi.nlm.nih.gov/pmc/articles/PMC3967127/

Sleep Foundation. (2025). *How blue light affects kids' sleep.* https://www.sleepfoundation.org/children-and-sleep/how-blue-light-affects-kids-sleep

Steare, T., Gutiérrez Muñoz, C., Sullivan, A., & Lewis, G. (2023). The association between academic pressure and adolescent mental health problems: A systematic review. *Journal of Affective Disorders, 339*, 302–317. https://doi.org/10.1016/j.jad.2023.07.028

Taylor, J. J., & Hamilton, L. S. (2019, March 28). How do you measure social and emotional learning? *RAND Corporation.* https://www.rand.org/pubs/commentary/2019/03/how-do-you-measure-social-and-emotional-learning.html

Tu, X. (2021). The role of classroom culture and psychological safety in EFL students' engagement. *Frontiers in Psychology, 12,* Article 760903. https://doi.org/10.3389/fpsyg.2021.760903

U.S. Department of Education. (2020). *Parent and family digital learning guide*. Office of Educational Technology. https://www.education.nh.gov/sites/g/files/ehbemt326/file s/inline-documents/sonh/parent-and-family-digital-learning-guide.pdf

U.S. Department of Health and Human Services. (2023, May 3). *Our epidemic of loneliness and isolation: The U.S. Surgeon General's Advisory on the healing effects of social connection and community* [PDF]. https://www.hhs.gov/sites/default/files/surgeon-general-social-connection-advisory.pdf

U.S. Department of Health and Human Services. (2023, May 23). *Social Media and Youth Mental Health: The U.S. Surgeon General's Advisory* [PDF]. https://www.hhs.gov/sites/default/files/sg-youth-mental-health-social-media-advisory.pdf

U.S. Department of Health and Human Services, Centers for Disease Control and Prevention. (2024, April 3). *Health benefits of physical activity for children.* https://www.cdc.gov/physical-activity-basics/health-benefits/children.html

U.S. Department of Health and Human Services, StopBullying.gov. (n.d.). *How to prevent cyberbullying: A guide for parents, caregivers, and youth* [PDF]. https://www.stopbullying.gov/sites/default/files/documents /Cyberbullying%20Guide%20Final%20508.pdf

Wilson, B. J., Petaja, H., Yun, J., King, K., Berg, J., Kremmel, L., & Cook, D. (2014). Parental emotion coaching:

Associations with self-regulation in aggressive/rejected and low-aggressive/popular children. *Child & Family Behavior Therapy, 36*(2), 81–106. https://doi.org/10.1080/07317107.2014.910731

World Health Organization. (2020). *WHO guidelines on physical activity and sedentary behaviour.* World Health Organization. https://www.ncbi.nlm.nih.gov/books/NBK566046/

World Health Organization. (2020). *Guidelines on mental health promotive and preventive interventions for adolescents: Helping adolescents thrive* [PDF]. https://www.who.int/publications/i/item/9789240011854

Yeager, D. S., Hanselman, P., Walton, G. M., Murray, J. S., Crosnoe, R., Muller, C., Tipton, E., Schneider, B., Hulleman, C. S., Hinojosa, C. P., Paunesku, D., Romero, C., Flint, K., Roberts, A., Trott, J., Iachan, R., Buontempo, J., Yang, S. M., Carvalho, C. M., Hahn, P. R., Gopalan, M., Mhatre, P., Ferguson, R., Duckworth, A. L., & Dweck, C. S. (2019). A national experiment reveals where a growth mindset improves achievement. *Nature, 573*(7774), 364–369. https://doi.org/10.1038/s41586-019-1466-y

Yeager, D. S., & Dweck, C. S. (2020). What can be learned from growth mindset controversies? *American Psychologist, 75*(9), 1269–1284. https://doi.org/10.1037/amp0000794

Zenner, C., Herrnleben-Kurz, S., & Walach, H. (2014). Mindfulness-based interventions in schools—A systematic review and meta-analysis. *Frontiers in Psychology, 5,* 603. https://doi.org/10.3389/fpsyg.2014.00603

Zimmerman, B. J. (2002). Becoming a self-regulated learner: An overview. *Theory Into Practice, 41*(2), 64–70. https://doi.org/10.1207/s15430421tip4102_2

www.ingramcontent.com/pod-product-compliance
Lightning Source LLC
Chambersburg PA
CBHW052353030726
47602CB00001B/9